Bridging the English Learner Achievement Gap

Bridging the English Learner Achievement Gap

Essential Lessons for School Leaders

Ray Garcia

TEACHERS COLLEGE PRESS

Teachers College
Columbia University
New York and London

Published by Teachers College Press, 1234 Amsterdam Avenue,
New York, NY 10027

Copyright © 2012 by Teachers College, Columbia University

All rights reserved. No part of this publication may be reproduced or transmitted in any form or by any means, electronic or mechanical, including photocopy, or any information storage and retrieval system, without permission from the publisher.

Library of Congress Cataloging-in-Publication Data

Garcia, Ray.
Bridging the English learner achievement gap : essential lessons for school leaders / Ray Garcia.
p. cm.
Includes bibliographical references and index.
ISBN 978-0-8077-5360-6 (pbk. : alk. paper)
ISBN 978-0-8077-5361-3 (hardcover : alk. paper)
1. English language—Study and teaching—Foreign speakers.2. Limited English proficient students—United States. 3. Academic achievement. 4. School administrators—United States. I. Title.
PE1128.A2G276 2012
428.0071'073—dc23

2012030591

ISBN 978-0-8077-5360-6 (paperback)
ISBN 978-0-8077-5361-3 (hardcover)

Printed on acid-free paper
Manufactured in the United States of America

19 18 17 16 15 14 13 12 8 7 6 5 4 3 2 1

Contents

Preface

Approximately 55.2 million students and more than 94,000 K–12 schools make up the public education system in this country, charged with producing the workforce needed to compete in a global economy. Increasingly, these schools are enrolling students whose primary language is not English. This evolving makeup of the student population has drawn attention to the prevailing student achievement gap between English learners and English-proficient students. Historically, the academic performance of English learners has been lower than that of other subgroups, and the achievement gap has narrowed little over the years in spite of decades of school reform.

The fundamental premise of this book is the sustainability of broad-based English learner school reform. The common thread is the unwrapping of organizational structures and their accompanying leadership skills to ensure the sustainability of English learner reform. This work consciously shies away from the provision of a cafeteria-style menu of English learner programs that could be considered for reform. Instead, this work focuses on the examination of deeper fundamental school structures required to ensure English learner success, all the while guiding the school leader in handling the reform terrain deftly. The intention is quite simplistic: structural reform that has an outsize effect on the classroom.

This book highlights the leadership challenge of meeting the academic needs of English learners in the context of school reform. Undergirding this theme is the historical trend of schools' inability to sustain reform. To address the sustainability dilemma, this text highlights sustainability indicators in the sustainability framework as a leadership tool for understanding and subsequently navigating school reform. The core chapters provide a progressive series of tools, exercises, and rubrics that engage the school leader in analyzing and developing discussions about English learner challenges in the context of sustaining school reform. With the emphasis throughout on English learner challenges, this book uses the sustainability framework as a venue to explore reform efforts in relation to closing the prevalent achievement gap of English learners in schools. By explicitly blending the two parallel threads, English learner challenges and the sustainability framework, this book offers insightful lessons about the required skill sets of school leaders as they go about the day-to-day routines of tackling school reform.

This work offers compelling as well as unique perspectives on the topic of reform sustainability as it pertains to impacting English learners. Using the challenges posed by the prevailing English learner student achievement gap as a reform theme, Chapters 1 and 2 engage the reader on a path toward understanding the magnitude of the English learner population in schools, the prevalence of the English learner achievement gap, as well as a profile of the historical failure of reform efforts. Through the introduction of the broad contours of the sustainability framework as a tool for understanding reform sustainability, this section helps the reader interpret reform implementation as well as comprehend the significance of building school readiness for sustainable English learner reform.

Chapters 3 through 8 profile the six English learner challenges through a deep examination of each of the challenges juxtaposed the indicators in the sustainability framework. A chapter is dedicated to each of the six English learner challenges and each chapter is dovetailed to a sustainability indicator. Hosting the core chapters, this section sharpens the picture for the school leader on how to use the sustainability framework for thinking about the fundamentals of school reform.

Last, Chapter 9 methodically establishes a leader's urging to undertake a calculated approach for selecting, sequencing, and delivering effective reform through a comprehensive model for instructional improvement for English learners. Through the examination of organizational structures from both the micro and the macro perspectives, this chapter synthesizes the salient points highlighted in the preceding chapters and brings it all together coherently for the school leader. This model offers suggestions for redesigning entire school systems and impacting the quality of instruction for English learners in the classroom. Recognizing that many school leaders with English learner populations lack the training on the basics of second language acquisition programming, this chapter maps out a practical course of action.

This book adds to the current practice of school reform by highlighting the missing, practical variable to the realization of reform sustainability: how to understand the dynamics of and subsequently sustain school reform for English learner success. The topics outlined in this work actively engage the school leader in understanding the needs of the English learner population as well as the organizational structures needed for school reform to anchor.

SPECIAL FEATURES

Certain elements are included in this work to help the reader experience different kinds of learning other than that when just reading the text:

- A Test Your Knowledge exercise culminates every section, offering the reader a series of reflective questions useful in enhancing practice.
- The Leadership Compass segments provide insights in developing leadership capabilities in sustaining English learner school reform.
- Application Exercises at the end of each chapter provide starting points for conversations with school staff.
- Rubrics in the core chapters facilitate dialogues for school leaders on a school's progress in English learner programming.

Acknowledgments

My appreciation is extended to the countless dedicated teachers and school leaders who have crossed my path in my educational career. Their commitment and insights have been instrumental in realizing this work. I specifically express my gratitude to the teachers and administrators in the Santa Clara Unified School District who have tremendously influenced this book, especially Lisa Cesario, Kris Stanga, Mary Kay Going, Shannon Potts, and Bobbie Plough.

I am grateful to my university colleagues whose guidance and comments added so much to the formulation of the vision for this project. I continue to appreciate Paula Lopez, whose keen eye for detail help make this book a reality.

My family has had an immeasurable influence on my thinking over the years. I owe so much, in every way, to my two sisters, Lina and Rosario, and my brother, Freddie, whose relentless support and ongoing encouragement have never wavered. They are the foundation of my very being.

Finally, my heartfelt appreciation is extended to the thousands of English learners in this country's public schools, whose commonly overseen subtle thirst to succeed academically is the catalyst behind this work. They now have a voice.

1

Educational Reform and the English Learner Achievement Gap

Minimal Impact to Show

> *Amidst the sweeping changes in the enterprise of teaching and learning, English language learners ... are one subgroup of students that require special attention, particularly because of their growing numbers and low-performance relative to their non-ELL peers. For schools, improving academic outcomes for ELLs is a litmus test for whether teachers are meeting their charge to truly leave no child behind. It is precisely in these times of change that opportunities arise for implementing purposeful teacher effectiveness initiatives that have promise for improving outcomes among the nation's least well-served students. (Samson and Collins, 2012, p. 1)*

The complexity of the public schools' organizational structure poses tremendous challenges in meeting the academic demands of an evolving makeup of the student population. According to Short and Fitzsimmons (2007), in virtually every part of the country, schools are expanding enrollments of students whose primary language is not English. Rising numbers of immigrants and other demographic trends make it clear that the nation can no longer afford to ignore the pressing needs of the English learners in public schools. These demographic changes have drawn attention to a linguistic achievement gap: the difference in academic performance between English-proficient students and English learners (Thomas & Collier, 2002).

This escalating phenomenon is not new to educators. Demographers have been predicting this change for decades. At the close of the 20th century, Hatch (1998) warns that the U.S. public education system was daunted by the chronic problem that children were experiencing differential levels of academic success distributed along race and social class. Unfortunately, the student achievement gap has become the norm for many schools in this country. Add to the quagmire the fact that despite countless school reform efforts during the last 3 decades, the achievement gap is more pronounced among certain groups of students. Inarguably, educators are faced with a rude awakening to the inability of school systems to sustain reform efforts for sufficient duration to realize an impact on student achievement. The state of the unsustainability of school reform, coupled with a pervasive English learner achievement gap, has now reached a crisis level in this country. The nation's educational system stands at a precipice!

This chapter covers the following:

- The evolving makeup of the public school system's student population;
- The characteristics of English learners in public schools;
- How the achievement gap is exacerbated for English learners; and
- The six challenges of English learner programming.

The structural complexity facing the nation's public school system is illustrated in Figure 1.1. There are three cogwheels at play that must be addressed simultaneously if educators are to narrow the achievement gap. Schools in this country are faced with a changing student population and, with it, an accompanying and widening student achievement gap that in turn appears to be the catalyst for the driving waves of school reform efforts that subsequently have done little to improve student achievement. By all indications, the public school system is caught in a vicious cycle.

Figure 1.1. The Cogwheels of School Reform

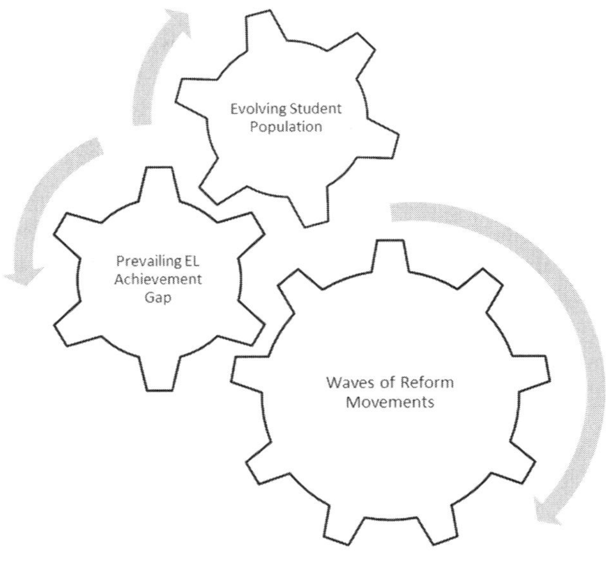

This book is about showing school leaders how to synchronize the cogwheels so that the synergy exerted from the motions work in favor of, not against, school improvement efforts. Why? The answer to this question is frankly: because many school leaders with English learner populations lack the background or training on the basics of second language acquisition programming. This work will help school leaders see how success is possible by facing the challenges head on and developing a deeper understanding of how to address them.

A poignant point about reform sustainability merits discussion at this juncture. As will be shown later in this chapter and throughout this book, reforms have escalated to enormous proportions in this country's public schools. Efforts to sustain them, however, have lagged behind. Partly due to the political pressures to close the achievement gap, the educational system is seeing an emerging consensus on the need to address reform sustainability in schools.

EVOLVING MAKEUP OF STUDENT POPULATION

To understand the fundamental challenges in public education today, we must understand their inception. In the past 30 years, the immigration movement in the United States has posed a plethora of unanticipated consequences for the educational system. The ripple effects of the immigration tsunami are rapidly changing the face, color, and texture of the nation's schools. With this evolution come enormous challenges posed to the educational systems. This section explores the evolving makeup of the student population through an investigation of the demographic changes in schools.

Over the last 3 decades, the English learner population has exploded relative to the English-only population in the United States (Rumberger, 2006). The English learner population increased by 130%, while the English-only population actually declined by 1.3%. In other words, the 5 million additional school-age children in the United States were English learners. U.S. Census data (see Figure 1.2) indicate there were 10.5 million children between 5 and 17 years old living in the United States in 2005 who spoke a language other than English, which represents 20% of the school-age population. As a group, English learners represent one of the fastest-growing groups among the school-age population in this nation. The U.S. Department of Education (2005) defines English learners as national-origin-minority students who are limited English proficient.

The nation's growth pattern shows only part of the picture. The geographic distribution of English learners offers another perspective. Demographers have argued that the English learner population is not evenly distributed across geographic regions in this country. Batalova, Fix, and

Figure 1.2. Linguistic Minority in the United States, 1980–2005

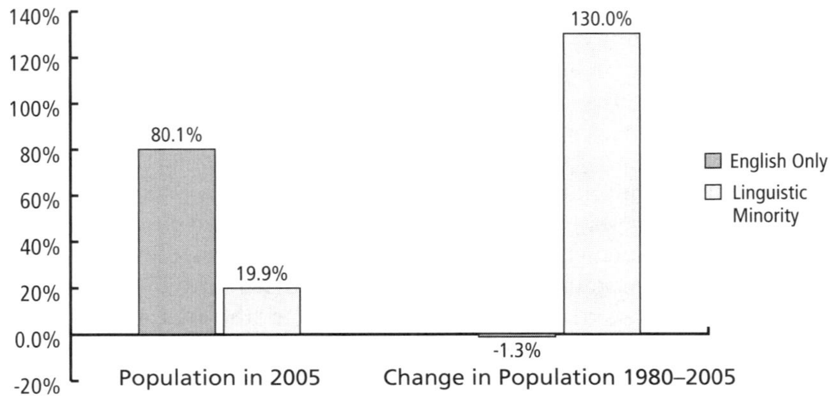

Reprinted from U.S. Bureau of the Census, *1980 Census of the Populatin,* Volume 1, Characteristics of the population. Chapters C/D, Detailed social and economic characteristics, Parts 1 and 6 (Washington, DC: U.S. Bureau of the Census, 1983); U.S. Bureau of the Census, 2005, American Community Survey. Retrieved from http://www.census.gov/acs/www/index.html

Murray (2005) found that in 2000, although five of the six top immigration states—California, Texas, New York, Florida, and Illinois—accounted for over 60% of all English learners in grades 6 through 12, the states with the fastest-growing numbers of English learners were different. Interestingly, North Carolina saw a 500% increase between 1993 and 2003. Colorado, Nevada, Nebraska, Oregon, Georgia, and Indiana each had more than 200% increases in that time period.

Additionally, demographers point out that while the absolute numbers of English learners in states such as North Carolina, Colorado, Oregon, Nevada, and Indiana are small compared with those in more traditional immigration states (California, Texas, Florida, and Illinois), the growth, nevertheless, has been quite rapid. It is these growing rates that raise concerns for school leaders about the resource readiness of schools (e.g., trained teachers, language support programs, curricula, and materials) and infrastructures to ensure that English learners have appropriate and effective academic and language instruction.

Understanding the student demographic shift in public schools recalibrates the approach to closing the achievement gap. Assuming that current trends continue, by the next decade it is projected that an overwhelming 30% of the school-age population in the United States will be English learners (Francis, Rivera, Lesaux, Kieffer, & Rivera, 2006). If English learners are forecasted to make up one-third of all students, then it behooves school leaders to take a proactive stance in preparing for this shift. The next section examines the student achievement gap of English learners and its implications for school leaders.

Test Your Knowledge

Until put to paper, many educators are unaware of the gradual change in their school or district student population. It is important to be familiar with the numbers of English learners, how they compare with national or regional figures, and what they mean.

1. What is the ethnic makeup of your student population?
2. Which group reflects the highest academic performance? Which group reflects the lowest?
3. What, in your opinion, accounts for this variance in academic performance?

CHARACTERISTICS OF ENGLISH LEARNERS

There are several subtle dynamics at play with English learners in schools. A research report by Center for Public Education (2007) found that a unique characteristic of the English learner subgroup is its instability. Students who learn English well enough to pass language proficiency tests move out of the subgroup, as new students who do not pass the test move in. This fluid trait has implications for accountability in schools. The success—or failure—of English learners can "count double" or, in some cases, "count triple" (in adequate yearly progress [AYP] calculations) because a student within an English learner classification may also belong to other subgroups (e.g., ethnic group, special education, free and reduced-priced lunch). The phrase "triple-dippers" will appear in subsequent chapters in this book.

The other subtle dynamic that characterizes English learners is the fact that the English learner label masks an enormous diversity. For example, the National Clearinghouse for English Language Acquisition and Language Instruction Educational Programs (2007) identified Spanish as the first language for 79% of English learners in the United States, with the Asian languages a distant second. Other English learners may speak any one of more than 400 languages found in public schools today. Additionally, English learners vary in their English proficiency levels and individual characteristics. In practical terms, this means that some urban classrooms in this country are populated with English learners speaking up to five different languages at varying levels of proficiency. This complex equation is what puzzles leaders in their school improvement efforts in the midst of intensifying accountability systems.

To help deepen an understanding of English learners, research has classified three English learner cohorts, defined on the basis of length of residency and schooling prior to immigration. In California, for example, the largest group comprises long-term English learners, who make up approximately two-thirds of the English learner population in the state's schools. The remainder of the English learner population is made up of recent immigrants with either low or high levels of previous schooling (Freeman, Freeman, & Mercuri, 2002). Dealing with the vast needs of these three cohorts is puzzling to practitioners and academics alike. Figure 1.3 outlines the characteristics and academic needs of these three cohorts of English learners.

The academic and linguistic requirements of each of the three cohorts are unique. Recent immigrants with significant amounts of previous schooling have mastered grade-level academic content and often require instruction only in English literacy skills. Having missed more than 1 year of academic instruction in their home country, recent immigrants with limited schooling require literacy skill development and content-area instruction in order to access the high school curriculum. Schooled primarily in the United States, long-term English learners are generally orally proficient but have poor reading and writing skills and little control of academic English (Faltis & Wolfe, 1999). Many long-term English learners are unable to exit from English language development programs because their academic achievement is not at grade level (Linquanti, 2001). Regardless of the academic and linguistic needs of each cohort, program displacement and poor monitoring

Figure 1.3. English Learner Cohorts and Defining Needs

Cohort 1 Recent Immigrants with Schooling	Cohort 2 Recent Immigrants with Limited Schooling	Cohort 3 Long-Term English Learners
• Have mastered academic content • Require instruction in English literacy skills	• Require literacy skills development • Require content-area instruction	• Generally orally proficient but lack reading & writing skills • Little control of academic English

of English learners limits access to academic and linguistic models and input. Placement in low-track classes contributes to the perception of English learners as "limited": limited in language, limited in knowledge, limited in skills, and limited in cultural competencies (Callahan, 2005).

In these cohorts, about 44% of the English language learners enrolled in U.S. middle and high schools, and 24 percent of English learners in elementary schools, were born outside the United States, according to 2000 census data. Students who are new not only to the language but also to the United States—and sometimes to formal schooling itself—present a unique set of difficulties, described among English learners as a period of sociocultural adjustment or "uprooting" in which immigrant students may experience depression or confusion due to their inability to communicate and may go through a "silent stage." This adjustment period may last 1 to 2 years (Francis et al., 2006).

At kindergarten entry, Rutherford (2006) found that English learner children of immigrants had significantly lower scores on the Oral Language Development Scale (which assesses oral English language ability) and on "school readiness" math scores than English learner children whose parents had been born in the United States. On these same assessments, Hispanic English learners scored significantly lower than other racial/ethnic groups. The Center on Instruction notes that immigrant English learners who enter U.S. schools at the secondary level are trying to learn academic content while simultaneously learning conversational and academic English in its oral and written forms and adjusting to a new culture and new school routines (Edvantia, 2007).

PREVAILING STUDENT ACHIEVEMENT GAP

That there is a race gap in educational achievement in public schools is not news. Large numbers of the nation's children leave school, with and without high school diplomas, barely able to read, write, and do simple math. But the failures of the schools are not evenly distributed. They fall disproportionately on students of color. Even when parents' income and wealth is comparable, African Americans, Native Americans, Latinos, and immigrants for whom English is not a first language lag behind English-speaking, native-born, White students. The evidence for the gap has been documented repeatedly by the usual measures. These include dropout rates and relative numbers of students who take the Advanced Placement examination, who are enrolled in the top academic and "gifted" classes, and/or are admitted to higher-status secondary schools, colleges, and graduate and professional programs. And last but not least are the discrepancies in scores on standardized tests of academic achievement, on which teachers' and students' fates so heavily depend (Center on Education Policy, 2009a).

The achievement gap for English learners is most blatant when looking at student performance at the national level. For starters, Abedi and Dietel (2004) report that English learners receive lower grades in school and have higher dropout rates than other students. Historically, the academic performance of English learners has been lower than that of other subgroups, and the achievement gap has narrowed little over the years. The authors use National Assessment of Educational Progress (NAEP) data to demonstrate the substantial and persistent English learner gap in both reading and math across grade levels. To magnify the extent of the gap, Figure 1.4 illustrates how 12th-grade English learners scored below the 8th-grade English native speakers in reading. In math, 8th-grade English learners scored slightly above the 4th-grade native speakers.

Figure 1.4. English Learner and English Native Speaker NAEP Performance

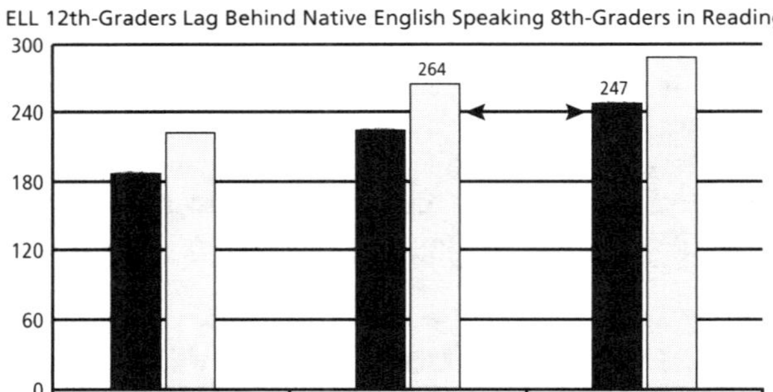

	4th	8th	12th
■ *English Learner*	187	224	247
□ *Non English Learner*	222	264	288

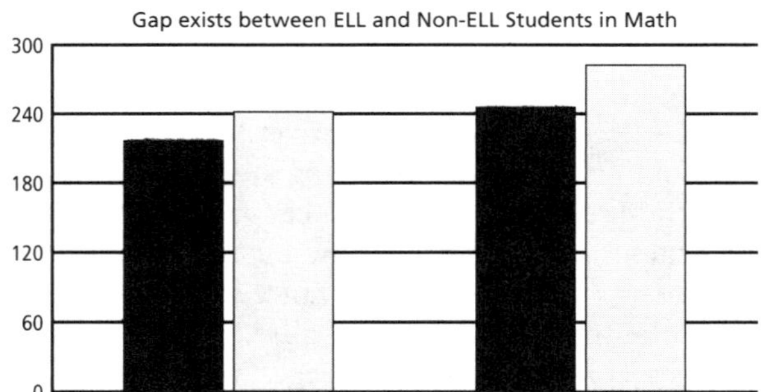

	4th	12th
■ *English Learner*	217	246
□ *Non English Learner*	242	283

Source: 2005 NAEP–Reading, www.nces.ed.gov/nationsreportcard. Includes ELL students who could be assessed with accommodations.

In California, one of the largest English learner–populated states, the gap takes on a new feel. An investigation into the performance of English learners in English language arts in the state's annual standardized test reveals that the academic achievement of English learners, particularly those who are not yet proficient in English, lags far behind children from English-only backgrounds. For example, Figure 1.5 shows the percentage of students scoring at the proficient level on the California Standards Test in English language arts in 2009 by language background. Only 39% of English learners scored at the proficient level in 2nd grade compared with 61% of the English-only students in the same grade level—a gap difference of 22 percentage points. The gap doubles by the time the English learner has reached high school. An astonishing 5% of the English learners scored at the proficiency level at the 11th grade in English language arts, compared with their English-only counterparts, who scored at the 47% proficiency level. Clearly, there is a downward trend in the academic performance of English learners as they progress through secondary schools.

Disturbingly, California schools failed to make a significant dent in a historically immovable achievement gap—one that leaves Black and Hispanic students lagging well behind their White and Asian peers. Based on

Figure 1.5. California's 2009 Achievement Gap in English Language Arts

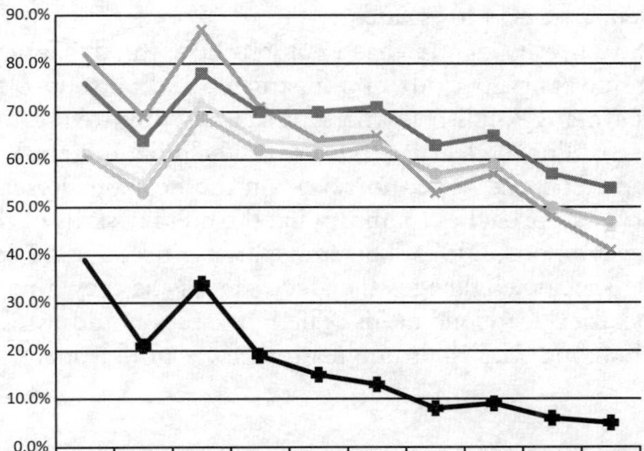

	2nd	3rd	4th	5th	6th	7th	8th	9th	10th	11th
English Only	61%	53%	69%	62%	61%	63%	57%	59%	50%	47%
Initially Fluent English Proficient	76%	64%	78%	70%	70%	71%	63%	65%	57%	54%
Fluent-English Proficient and EO	62%	55%	72%	64%	63%	64%	56%	59%	50%	46%
Reclassified Fluent English Proficient	82%	69%	87%	71%	64%	65%	53%	57%	48%	41%
English Learner	39%	21%	34%	19%	15%	13%	8%	9%	6%	5%

Source: California Department of Education, Dataquest. (n.d.).

the rate of improvement from 2003 to 2009, it would take up to 105 years to close the White/Hispanic achievement gap (*San Francisco Chronicle*, 08/19/09). With the accountability pressure increasing in schools today, there is no shortage of tension among leaders in the failing schools of the urgency to meet the needs of English learners in this country.

One of the most prevalent causes of the gap between English learners and non-English learners is the English learners' inability to grasp academic language in content areas (math, science, and social studies). Beyond simply a matter of vocabulary learning, academic language is defined as cognitively demanding, its most obvious feature being that it is relatively de-contextualized. It relies on broad knowledge of words, phraseology, grammar, discourse structure, and pragmatic conventions for expression, understanding, and interpretation (Cummins, 1984). Chapter 6 delves into more detail on the role and importance of academic language for English learners.

Although many of these English learners typically have good conversational English skills, they lack much of the academic language that is central to success with content-area text. For example, in several studies with English learners in the elementary and middle school years, Biancarosa and Snow (2006) found that these students' academic language levels are often well below average, sometimes with a group average as low as the 20th percentile. Such low vocabulary levels are insufficient to support effective reading comprehension and writing, and in turn have a negative impact on overall academic success. Mastery of academic language is inarguably the key to content-area learning and the single most important determinant of academic success for students.

So far, this chapter has explored how the dynamics of instability, language diversity, periods of adjustment, and mastery of academic language plague many English learners in schools. Improving the academic performance of English learners is an overwhelming undertaking for many school leaders. There is hope, however, on the horizon. Researchers are bringing clarity to approaches to improving the literacy skills of these students (Short & Fitzsimmons, 2007). This transparency becomes more evident by looking at the specific challenges that face schools as they attempt to address English learner academic needs. The next section addresses these challenges in depth, along with their implications for school leaders.

Test Your Knowledge

Trace the performance of your English learners: The achievement gap is, in and of itself, just the tip of the iceberg. In other words, there are many complexities undergirding the gap. Take a thorough examination of the English learners in your school.

1. Do you find the mobility rate of English learners to be higher than other student groups?
2. How many different languages are spoken by your English learners? How do your teachers reconcile this challenge in their classroom?
3. Are your English learners disproportionately receiving lower grades in the classrooms when compared with their native-English-speaking counterparts?

THE SIX CHALLENGES OF ENGLISH LEARNER PROGRAMMING

The prevailing gap in the English learner population requires a deeper examination of the problems posed in meeting the needs of these students. As the previous section showed, English learners present a unique set of challenges to school leaders because of the prominent role played by academic language proficiency while simultaneously mastering content-area knowledge. While their native-English-speaking counterparts are focusing on learning content knowledge and skills, English learners are struggling with a dual challenge: learning the same content while simultaneously acquiring English language proficiency. In theory, this dual challenge is plausible. In actual practice, however, this scenario offers a totally different picture. Figure 1.6 illustrates the four dimensions of English language development (listening, speaking, reading, and writing) and the complexity that the English learner must navigate and master in order to make sense of subject-matter content.

As discussed earlier, a cohort 1 (Recent Immigrants with Schooling) English learner would require more emphasis on the reading and writing dimensions of the English language development (ELD) Model. A cohort 2 (Recent Immigrant with Limited Schooling) English learner would require learning experiences that concentrate on the speaking and reading dimensions while a cohort 3 English learner would do well with exposure to the reading and writing dimensions of the ELD model. It is important to remember that these emphases on ELD are occurring simultaneously while the English learner is attempting to master the content.

Although the ELD model reflects sound approaches to the English Language development of English learners, it is also good, sound literacy development for all students. In other words, the ELD model is a mirror image of the dimensions of literacy development.

Figure 1.6. Four Dimensions of English Language Development Model

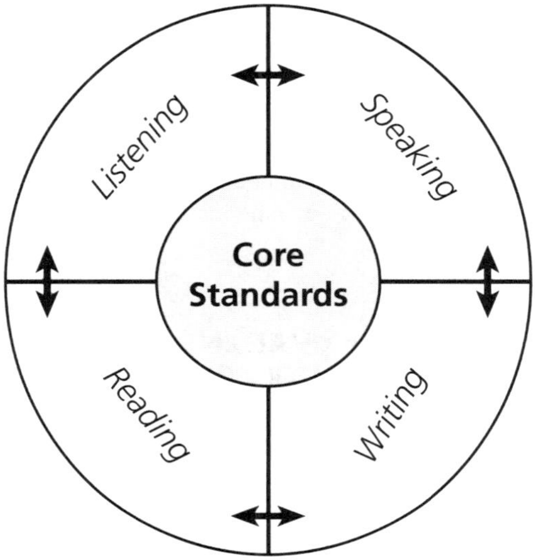

Literacy development in English learners is a daunting challenge for schools with growing populations of English learners. Francis et al. (2006) show that although many factors can facilitate second language literacy acquisition, developing literacy in a second language is not an easy undertaking. While simultaneously developing conversational ability and basic reading skills, English learners must quickly begin to develop oral and written academic language skills for the development of academic knowledge and success in content-area classrooms. Chapter 7 is dedicated entirely to addressing the issues related to literacy development in English learners.

Having a sound understanding of English language development provides a backdrop to understanding the challenges that face English learners in schools. To bring the issues and challenges confronting English learners to the forefront, the Center for Applied Linguistics convened a panel of researchers, policymakers, and practitioners working in the field. With a focus on literacy development, the panel spelled out a catalog of six major challenges to improving English learner performance (Short & Fitzsimmons, 2007):

1. *Identification, program placement, & tracking academic progress:* Current identification measures do not often provide the requisite information for accurate English learner placement. Once the

student is identified, English learner programs often place students in modified instruction, which translates to less linguistically and academically rigorous instruction than mainstream instruction. In these displaced environments, English learners fail to acquire the grade-level academic and linguistic competency necessary to exit English learner/language proficiency programs (LEP).

2. *Appropriate assessments*: There is a need to improve assessments for determining English learners' native language abilities, their progress in English language development, and their mastery of academic language in content areas.
3. *Flexible program options*: English learners need programs that are age-appropriate, motivating, and designed with realistic second language and literacy development expectations. The traditional school model does not seem to favor English learners.
4. *Research-based instructional strategies*: The research on effective instruction with English learners is lacking. Lectures and worksheets do not provide effective learning scaffolding for English learners. The instructional strategies for English learners should account for the students' second language development as well as their content-knowledge requirements.
5. *Coherent literacy approach*: The panel found that instructional strategies that are effective with native English speakers do not have as positive a learning impact on language minority students, and that instruction in the key components of reading is necessary but not sufficient for teaching language minority students to read and write proficiently in English.
6. *Staff capacity*: Many school leaders and teachers lack training in integrating language instruction in their content lessons. Skillful teachers trained in literacy development should be a focus for schools with large English learner populations. These teachers will in turn help English learners develop literacy skills in the content areas in their second language.

Either in isolation or collectively, these challenges pose tremendous implications for educational leaders as they attempt to work with their teaching staff in meeting the academic as well as language proficiency needs of English learners. Table 1.1 reflects a synthesis of these challenges supplemented with the emerging issues undergirding each challenge, and the leadership mandates required to address each challenge. It should be noted that each of these challenges is addressed in depth in the core chapters that follow.

Table 1.1. Six Challenges for Improving English Learner Performance

English Learner Challenge	Emerging Issue	Leadership Mandates
1. Identification, Program Placement, and Tracking Academic Progress	Is the placement of English learners in English language development programs effective? What evidence proves this?	The leader regularly monitors the development of English language proficiency in English learners as well as mastery of academic language in content areas, ensuring appropriate program placement.
2. Appropriate Assessments	Are current assessments effectively gauging English language development as well as mastery of academic language in content areas?	The leader uses formative as well as summative assessment data to ensure English learners are mastering academic vocabulary in the content areas.
3. Flexible Program Options	Is there flexibility in the current school structure/ program, allowing English learners to enter and exit readily? Are some programs a hindrance to English learners?	The leader ensures flexibility in programs serving English learners by identifying appropriate programs that accelerate English language development and progress in content areas. An indicator of flexibility is the ease with which English learners enter and exit the programs.
4. Research-based Instructional Strategies	Are the current classroom instructional strategies embedding English language development through their content instruction?	The leader is versed in and ensures that classroom strategies provide effective learning scaffolds for English learners.

Table 1.1. (continued)

5. Coherent Literacy Approach	Are teachers versed in English learner literacy development?	The leader ensures that assessments are appropriate for measuring English learner literacy development.
6. Staff Capacity	Is literacy development for English learners a professional development focus?	The leader ensures an articulation between English language development teachers and content-area teachers with literacy development at its centerpiece.

Test Your Knowledge

English learners pose a unique set of challenges to a school partly because of the role played by the acquisition of academic language proficiency while mastering content.

1. What is your most prevalent emerging challenge with regard to English learners in your school?
2. How are you and your teachers addressing this issue? What interventions are in place?
3. What English learner achievement data give you the confidence that the interventions are effective?

This chapter has established that (1) there is an evolving makeup in the student population in the public schools in this country and that English learners comprise much of that evolution; (2) the English learner student population poses unique challenges to school leaders in that English language acquisition must be reconciled simultaneously while the student is mastering content standards; (3) the culprit for the failure to narrow the achievement gap is our lack of understanding of reform sustainability; and (4) the unveiling of the six challenges to improving English learner performance. The next chapter looks at examining the dynamics of school reform and furthering our understanding of reform sustainability.

Chapter 1 Application Exercises:
Framing the English Learner Challenges in the Context of the Student Achievement Gap

Individual Exercise A high-leverage strategy for improving English learner academic achievement is through the creation of frequent, common, and valid formative assessments that examine English language development in concert with mastery of academic language. Describe the monitoring system you have in place and approaches to sustaining it.

Team Exercise If your team's priority is to impact English learners, the obvious question is how. To what degree has your team examined, clarified, and agreed to the essential outcomes for your English learners? How does your team plan to sustain the momentum of your work?

School Exercise At your next schoolwide meeting, count off by threes into small groups. Working first individually and then with members of your small group, reflect on ways that teachers demonstrate commitment to a reform. Be specific about the reform and why the initiative has promoted learning for English learners in your school. Is there evidence that the reform has closed the achievement gap? Share findings with the larger group.

2

Understanding School Reform

The Sustainability Framework

> *Even the most optimistic person would have to admit that there has been little overall improvement in the quality of U.S. public education. State legislatures, the federal government, business and industry, and special interest and community groups have pumped billions of dollars into educational reform. They have spent countless hours in debate and strategy sessions and have added their voices to the groundswell of calls demanding better education. (Conzemius & O'Neill, 2001, p. 4)*

After more than a decade of higher academic standards, more test-based accountability, and expanded school choice, nearly one-fourth of U.S. schools are still "failing" by the standards of No Child Left Behind (Basken, 2006), and a disproportionate number of these schools serve America's poor and minority students (Rowan, Correnti, Miller, & Camburn, 2009). Nested within these failing schools is a rapidly growing population of students classified as English learners. English learners attend schools with common characteristics: low-performing, poor standardized test performance, high student–teacher ratios, high student enrollments, and high levels of students living in or near poverty (Fry, 2008). Additionally, these schools are defined by another subtle characteristic: a chronic nature of unsustainable school reform (Taylor, 2006). In other words, the type of schools that English learners attend lack the skill and/or the will to reform themselves sufficiently to narrow the achievement gap of low-performing subgroups.

Reform and sustainability are in a hyphenated relationship. What affects one side of the relationship eventually affects the other side as well. What throws this equation off-balance however, is the fact that sustainability is rarely factored in during the planning process by school reformers. Taylor (2006) posits that going through a reform effort without planning for sustainability will simply bring yet another wave of reform movement.

The researcher further argues that even reform efforts that have been shown to be successful will do little to address the pervasive achievement gap that blemishes our educational system unless we learn to better address sustainability issues.

This chapter focuses on understanding the dynamics of school reform and unveils a sustainability framework rich with indicators that leaders can consider as they work to sustain efforts to improve schools. This chapter explores the following topics:

- The dynamics of school reform;
- The concept of reform distortion;
- A historical profile of the waves of educational reform;
- The notion of sustainability; and
- An introduction to the sustainability framework.

The centerpiece of this chapter is the application of the sustainability framework as a tool for leaders to use in furthering their understanding of the sustainability of school reform to address English learner needs. The framework identifies research-based indicators (Taylor, 2006) shown to sustain reform efforts. This research demonstrates that sustainability is associated with an array of variables, but most of these variables are conceptually underpinned by the prominence of six identified variables in the research: 1) instructional leadership, 2) alignment, 3) teacher commitment, 4) sustained professional development, 5) teacher retention, and 6) school capacity.

Undergirding the foundation of reform sustainability is a comprehensive discussion of school reform. It is becoming more imperative for school leaders to be well versed in the elements and dynamics that make up educational reform.

UNDERSTANDING REFORM

Goodson (2001) writes that educational reform represents a coalition of interests and projects hosted under a common name at a particular point in time. Fundamentally, a reform can be considered an expression of people's values, beliefs, political opinions, and morals—embedded within a particular power context. Although school reforms carry both implicit and explicit assumptions about how educators, and particularly teachers, should work, these assumptions can provoke strong emotional reactions—and hence, resistance to or acceptance of a reform. The central point to consider here is that reform, like teaching itself, is primarily a human enterprise invested with emotional, intellectual, political, and moral implications (Little &

Bartlett, 2002). Understanding these essential principles of human behavior is critical to understanding why some reforms work effectively while others fail miserably. What this inconsistency conveys is that, ultimately, reforms are a rather personal matter. It behooves school leaders to consider the human dynamics as well as their implications.

U.S. public schools are in a highly reform-active period with mounting pressures on schools to show evidence of academic progress. Little (2001) says that the reform climate has moved from a relatively progressive mood to a starkly conservative one, from resource flexibility to resource controls, from open-ended invitations to restructure to uniform mandates centered on state standards and high-stakes testing. The escalating demands in student performance as called for by the No Child Left Behind federal legislation serve to validate this reform climate.

In this reform-frenzy era, educational reforms are migrating through an evolutionary process characterized by distinct growth phases. Conceptualizing the evolutionary phases of reform is key to enhancing an understanding of reforms and, subsequently, how to sustain them. Century and Levy (2002) identified three primary stages of reform evolution that advance school innovation from maintenance to sustainability. The demarcation boundaries between phases are fluid, with reforms rarely progressing consistently forward. Interestingly, within this migration, reforms advance, stall, slide back, contract, retrench, and then move ahead again. Conversely, some reforms see their demise at various stages of this same migration.

Called establishment, the initial phase focuses on the very concrete goals of the reform, making sure that they are well established, accepted, and working efficiently and predictably in schools. The establishment phase is considered the introduction of the reform via protocol and distribution of materials. Implementing professional development for both teachers and administrators is essential at this time.

The second developmental phase is maturation. The focus of this phase is on embedding the reform across the organization and arriving at a point where the reform is habitual. In other words, the reform is being accepted by the school culture. Maturation is considered to be the point where the reform has been absorbed by the school and has become part of the everyday operations of the staff.

The third phase of development is evolution. This third and final phase is the sustainability of the reform and the revamping of the initiative to construct a new set of goals. The hallmarks of the evolution phase are growth and improvement within a school as the goals of the reform are realized (Century & Levy, 2002). Figure 2.1 reflects a graphic representation of these evolutionary phases essential for school leaders' understanding of the planning and assessing of reforms in schools.

Figure 2.1. The Growth Phases of Reform

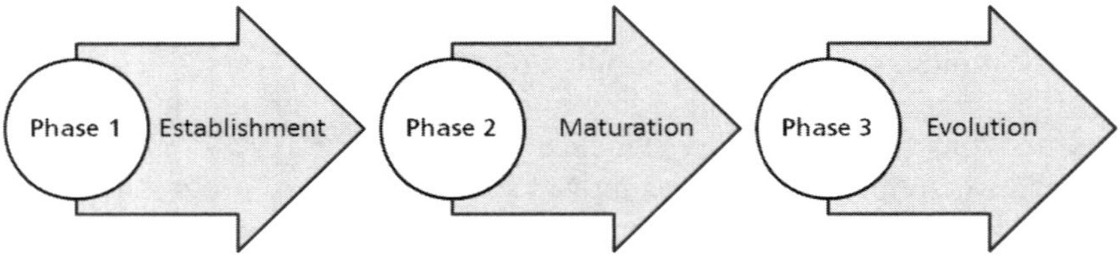

Implementation fidelity over time fuels a reform as it moves across the three phases in this model. Unfortunately, as will be shown later in this chapter, the school reform literature (Tyack & Cuban, 1995) generally indicates that very few school-reform efforts have the capacity to migrate into the Phase 3 scenario representing sustained implementation of reform.

Test Your Knowledge

The effective implementation of a reform is key to the success of the initiative. However, undergirding the implementation process is a wide array of human dynamics that require transparency. Using the Growth Phases of Reform graphic, reflect on the following questions:

1. What is your school's most prevalent initiative for addressing English learner academic needs?
2. Where is this initiative in the Growth Phases of Reform?
3. What factors have moved this reform to this level?
4. What is keeping this reform from moving forward?

SYSTEMIC REFORM DISTORTION

As reforms are evolving in their growth, they must pass through a variety of organizational boundaries, and at times, barriers, established by the bureaucratic nature of schools. Framing reform migration from an organizational perspective helps one understand the change process in schools. Noell and Gansle (2009) write that although there are important differences between changing the behavior of groups and changing the behavior of individuals, at a fundamental level, changing the behavior of schools begins by changing the behavior of a critical mass of individuals. Schoolwide reform, therefore, is about establishing behavioral change and subsequently sustaining that behavioral change.

Most reforms are inherently not systemic, because they focus on a part of a school as the unit of change. True systemic change requires substantial changes in all aspects of an educational system (e.g., policy, classroom practices, curriculum, assessment, and so forth) (Reigeluth, 1994). For change in education to be successful in dramatically improving learning for English learners, it will require a fundamental rethinking or mindset shift in the way learning is structured for children; it also will require a radical redesign of the entire educational system and its processes. This is simply another way of saying that the narrowing of the English learner achievement gap requires systemic reform in schools and not the piecemeal approaches that characterize most current reforms. Duffy, Rogerson, and Blick (2000) write:

> In the literature on school improvement, there are many reasons why schools need to be improved. In the same literature, there are many authors telling you what the outcomes of school improvement should be. Some of these models aim to improve individual school buildings, while others attempt to improve the curricula. Very few of them however, talk about how to redesign entire school systems for high performance. Most of what is described in the literature represents incremental, piecemeal change. (p. xvi)

Years ago, Cuban (1986) explained that reforms do not really change schools—that, quite the contrary, schools change reforms. Keefe and Amenta (2005) substantiated this argument by adding that schools have become increasingly obsolete. The organizational structure of the typical American school, the researchers argued, is antiquated and is becoming more and more outdated. The infrastructure of the public school system was developed when the country was building a blue-collar workforce and only a few students were expected to go to college. Although some evolution in curricula has occurred, the core belief systems remain relatively unchanged in schools. Reform sustainability requires attending to fundamental, deep-rooted, entrenched patterns in schools. Tending to the organizational environment in schools is essential to carrying out successful reform implementation.

The school environment has always been characterized by turbulence. Stricherz (2001) notes that education has been reformed again and again and again in the midst of chaotic work environments, and in some cases, reforms have been the culprits for causing the chaotic conditions. As will be noted later in this chapter, and as Crowson (2003) shows, there have been waves of reform where historical battles in education have ensured who pays, who benefits, who gets left behind, who controls, whose goals prevail, and who evaluates. As the nation has grown, each of its many (often turbulent) struggles in development has been thoroughly played out in the schools—including the schools' adaptations to waves of immigration, rural-to-urban migration, industrialization, civil unrest, revolutions in individual and group rights, economic ups and downs, technological developments, and cultural transformations. It is not hard to appreciate the common complaints of school leaders that the policy agenda in education tends perennially to be overcrowded, with too much on the administrative plate and too much frustration in getting things done.

Although turbulence in schools is not at all a new phenomenon, and indeed is a historical source of administrator and teacher complaints, the nation's schools are currently under significant alteration—they are neither more nor less turbulent than before, but different, and perhaps more cumulatively frustrating. Federal, state, local, and site levels are all present-day sources of much tension, indecision, concern, storminess, struggles (over issues from revenues to outcomes), and unfortunately, few victories (Crowson, 2003).

Thus far, this discussion has unveiled three salient points: 1) that reform in schools requires change in people's behavior; 2) that the very structure of schools themselves may not allow for reforms to be implemented effectively and/or efficiently; and 3) that these two elements serve as undercurrents day in and day out, causing organizational turbulence that undermines the very reform process. In this context of education reforms in turbulent work conditions, why are reforms so distorted that infiltrating the classroom is the exception and not the rule (Gu & Day, 2006)?

The problem of school reform has always been whether reform efforts can penetrate through the multiple levels of the educational system. Labaree (2007) asserts that the goal of any reform effort is ultimately to impact classroom practice. This is where reform ideas, if they succeed in passing through the machinery of the school system largely unscathed, need to pass through the door of the classroom in order to merge into the professional practice of teaching. The actors here, the author explains, are teachers, and the key issue is the extent to which these practitioners adopt or adapt the school reform. At this level is the instructional core of the educational enterprise, and reform success depends entirely on the capability and willingness of 3 million American public school teachers in 95,000 schools to take on the reform agenda and put it into practice in their classrooms. On the face of it, the sheer number, diversity, and geographical dispersion of these teachers and classrooms in the public school system suggests how difficult it is to effect reform at this level of the educational system. Research shows that it is extraordinarily hard for reformers to shape the practice of teaching in individual classrooms.

Figure 2.2 provides an illustration of how reform efforts become distorted as they make their way through the multitude of levels of a school.

Even when a reform has infiltrated the classroom walls, it is at this very juncture that reform is faced with its greatest challenge—teacher resistance. Reform distortion is further exacerbated by teachers' resistance to change. Because teachers in this country's public schools have seen the failure of one reform after another, they have built reform bubbles as a survival strategy to maintain some semblance of classroom stability. In other words, the organizational turbulence that is experienced by the classroom in today's schools is so intense that teachers' resistance to change may be simply a survival tactic. Teachers' perceptions or orientations of the world of school that surrounds them on a daily basis is the catalyst for this phenomenon.

In his seminal study, Lortie (1975) argued that the culture of public school teaching was characterized by three overlapping and mutually reinforcing teacher orientations that impede educational reform: presentism, conservatism, and individualism. Presentism, according to Lortie, refers to the overwhelming pressures of schools that kept teachers locked into short-term perspectives and unable or unwilling to envision or plan collaboratively for long-term, systemic change. Related to presentism, conservatism

Figure 2.2. The Reform Distortion Model

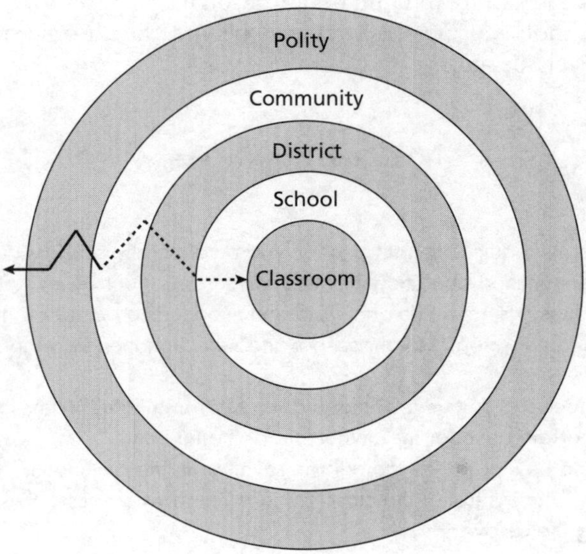

references teachers' mistrust of reform initiatives and their loyalty to established classroom practices that works for them regardless of research findings or pupil learning outcomes. Finally, individualism is manifested in teachers' preferences for working alone without the intrusion of colleagues or administrators in their own cellular classrooms.

Lortie (1975) argued that each of these three orientations are interwoven with and embedded in the others. From the teacher-orientation perspective, the major problem in school reform may reside not in governance issues, school and community relationships, or a given curriculum, significant as these may be. Rather, the researcher's work unveiled that an enormous impediment to school reform resides not in these contextual factors, but rather in the very core of teachers' own self-understandings of their work and its real meaning as a professional practice. Until educators and policymakers can find ways to break this fundamental source of resistance, the author held, reforms could never stand a chance of succeeding. Togneri and Anderson (2003) argued that so often reform efforts look at everything except how to help teachers help their students learn.

This section has shown that as reforms migrate through the multiple layers of the bureaucratic structure in schools, they are faced with barriers and challenges that dilute their very essence. Even when reforms infiltrate the classroom walls, it is there that they face their ultimate challenge. What is becoming clear to researchers and practitioners alike is that schools are suffering from the perils of reform stagnation. The institutional muscles in schools—the willingness to change when necessary—have atrophied (Elmore, 2000). The failure to build organizational structures to sustain reform is seen by school reformers as a culprit behind the chronic nature of the sustainability challenge.

Test Your Knowledge

Successful reforms require attending not only to bureaucratic barriers but also to deep-rooted, entrenched operational patterns in schools—our belief systems and how we run things. Using the Reform Distortion Model as a backdrop, trace the path of an English learner reform in your school and reflect on the following questions:

1. Where precisely, on this graphic, did the reform initiate? What implications does this origin pose for the ownership of the initiative?
2. Where and how long has the reform traveled on the continuum?
3. Has the reform infiltrated the classroom? If yes, how successfully? If no, what is causing the delay?

WAVES OF EDUCATIONAL REFORM

With the availability of standardized test scores on the Internet, a school's academic performance, or lack thereof, is at the public's fingertips, leading to national, state, and local governments' incessant demands for schools to increase student performance. As society urges more of schools in an era of diminishing resources, pressure for public school reform comes from the political, business, and private sectors. Flett and Wallace (2005) report that although there may be many calls for reform, successful reforms are far less frequent, and in some cases, failure is almost predictable. The factors contributing to successful reform in one scenario do not necessarily work in another.

Earlier segments in this book showed that the evolving English learner population in schools appears to be the student subgroup reflecting the widest disparity in student achievement performance. The chronic nature of the student achievement gap is haunting many schools in this country. In the past 3 decades, in a knee-jerk reaction to addressing the achievement gap, the education community has seen three major surges of reform efforts. The waves of educational reform can be categorized into three phases, as illustrated in Figure 2.3.

Educational historians lack consensus on the beginnings and endings of the reform waves that have characterized public education in the United States. However one demarcates these reform waves, there has been minimal progress in narrowing the student achievement gap.

In their exploration of the field of school improvement, Hopkins and Reynolds (2001) characterized these three phases in the evolution of school reform efforts. The first phase (1960s–1970s) was driven by the federal government's channeling of funds to individual schools to support teachers who worked with high-needs students, almost bypassing the district office. Other researchers, such as Fuhrman, Clune, and Elmore (1988), write that this

Figure 2.3. The Waves of Educational Reform Movements

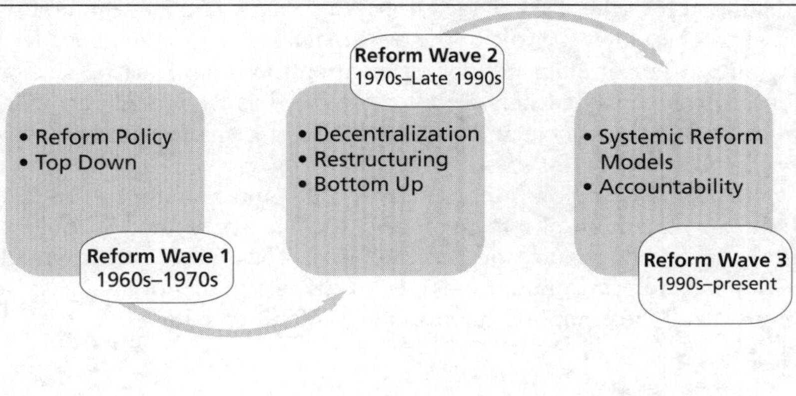

first wave was defined by several new trends in the enactment of reform policies. These researchers found increased levels of state activity in terms of the top-down school reform mandates in the form of graduation requirements, length of school year and school day, and mastery of basic skills. Interestingly, Fuhrman and colleagues also found little resistance to these top-down policies, as most districts were already in the process of reforming their practices.

During this first phase, public support for reform was strong, and the changes that states were called upon to make were within the capacity of districts and school personnel to achieve. Marks and Nance (2007) convey that in many cases, districts used state mandates as a catalyst for further reforms and—often with the help of state funding—as opportunities to achieve local objectives. As this reform movement was coming to a close, school districts were responding to local needs, and were engaged in policymaking, as well as interacting with other districts in terms of sharing and borrowing best practices. Given all these efforts, the student achievement gap showed little promise of narrowing.

The early 1970s saw the evolution of the second wave of education reform. In their exploration of change in schools, Harris and Chrispeels (2006) report that during this time, the school as a whole emerged as a significant factor as research on school and classroom effectiveness was brought to the forefront. This phase unearthed a deeper understanding of critical schoolwide characteristics that contributed to overall school effectiveness—an effort that came to be known as the effective schools movement.

The restructuring of schools was a major thrust during this phase. Policymakers and politicians alike called for localized and participatory decision-making as the focus for school improvement. Invariably, Marks and Louis (1997) recount, site-based management became the dominant feature of the second wave of school reform. Elmore (1993) characterized site-based management as a call for decentralization that diminished the influence of districts on schools. In many cases, the districts' influence on curriculum and instruction at the school site tended to be fragmented and ineffectual. It was during this phase that the role of the principal as an instructional leader for school improvement emerged, complementing the role of teachers as education professionals. Teachers were legitimatized as experts in curriculum, instruction, and assessment and were granted a voice in decision-making on school improvement efforts.

Chrispeels, Burke, Johnson, and Daly (2008) note that during this phase, schools saw a plethora of reform models, such as Accelerated Schools, Coalition of Essential Schools, and Success for All. These school-reform models were designed to bring about fundamental changes in school organizational structures, and most important, curriculum and instruction.

By the late 1990s, as the years of innovation showed little or no impact on the closing of the achievement gap, the third wave of reform began to incubate. With neither the first-wave nor the second-wave reform producing significant improvement in student achievement, policymakers rethought reform in systemic terms and, hence, the birth of the current, third wave of school reform. Characterized by systemic reform, this third wave aims at aligning and coordinating the components of the school as a system—policies, curriculum standards, and professional development. Conley (2003) reminds us that undergirding this third wave of reform is accountability for results, with individual states ranking, classifying, and even sanctioning districts for their student academic performance. The commonality among the states' accountability models is a direct focus on schools, which must meet performance standards and eliminate performance gaps. Keefe and Amenta (2005) point out that this increased accountability in schools advocates for longer school days, extended school years, fewer electives, high school exit exams, and competency standards.

The federal government has added its own take to the educational reform arena. In 2001, the U.S. Congress approved a reauthorization of the Elementary and Secondary Education Act, renaming it the No Child Left Behind Act (NCLB). This legislation includes a performance-based accountability system built around student test results. This increased emphasis on accountability represents an important change from past federal educational initiatives that focused primarily on the provision of services (Stecher & Kirby, 2004).

The impact of the three waves of reform movements, coupled with an accountability thrust, remains bleak. In their national study, Nichols, Glass, and Berliner (2006) found that in most states, high-stakes testing programs associated with accountability systems were ineffective in achieving their intended purposes, and caused severe unintended negative consequences. Over the past 3 decades, educational reform efforts in the United States have been peppered with educators' and politicians' rhetoric of their commitment that all children will learn. While in no way an indictment of this commitment, the startling actuality is that there has been little progress to measure. One could argue that this widespread commitment, coupled with considerable financial investments in education over this same period, should have resulted in sustained improvement of public school systems. The economic times facing the nation serve only to exacerbate the challenge of advancing school reform in an era of declining resources (Garcia, 2009). The achievement gap for English learners is still disturbing, with no clear solution in sight.

Three waves of reform movements in this country have had little impact on the student achievement gap. The common denominator is becoming progressively clear: Schools suffer from a chronic trait of unsustainable reform.

If this dilemma is to change, public schools must be responsive to what it takes to sustain school improvement. For some leaders, systematic customization of curriculum and instruction is the solution to sustaining school reform. For others, the need is to address the entrenched patterns in daily practice that are all too common in schools (Southworth & DuQuesnay, 2005). These issues are being called into question in the body of research on reform sustainability. The chronic challenge of sustaining school reform will be addressed in the section that follows.

A BRIEF HISTORY OF FAILED REFORMS

The three waves of reform draw a blatant picture of the history of unsustained reform in the U.S. public school system. In a study of Comprehensive School Reform (CSR), Taylor (2006) examined a sample of 395 urban, disadvantaged, low-achieving elementary and middle schools implementing reforms in 2001–2002 and found that nearly one-third of these schools ended their relationships with their program developers by the end of 2003–2004. In probing deeper, the researcher also found that of the 395 schools in 21 districts that were implementing reforms in 2001–2002, 73 (19%) schools had dropped or switched their reform before or during the following school year. In this same period, 13% of the schools reported dropping their program altogether, and 6% reported that they had dropped their reforms and switched to a different one.

The scope of unsustained reforms merits further validation. Berends, Kirby, Naftel, and McKelvey (2001) noted that at least 24% of the schools in their study ended their relationship with their reformer. In a study of one urban district, Datnow (2005) reported that after 3 years, reforms expired in 6 of the 13 schools under study. Another study by Academic Information Management, Inc. (2003) found that 25% (27 of 106) of the responding schools had discontinued their original reform by the 5th year after adoption. Evans, Baugh, Sheffer, Martin, and Scarentino (2004) found that 36% (28 of 78) of the schools visited 5 years after initial adoption of a reform were no longer implementing the reform. Noguera (2004) highlighted a study of ten schools in the Boston Public School System that were undertaking a variety of reform strategies. A closer look revealed an all too common pattern. The researcher discovered that the reform efforts were fragmented and managed ineffectively. Eight of the ten schools demonstrated no achievement gains. The chronic nature of unsustainable reform in schools is inarguable. It is this chronic trait in school reform that is contributing to the English learner achievement gap.

Providing a variety of perspectives, this segment has highlighted the inability of schools to sustain reform. Program after program and reform after reform have left school leaders cynical about sustainable school improvement. In many schools in this country, reform is perceived as a program du jour. Inarguably, school leaders are in need of a tool for enacting effective reform sustainability. The next section introduces a tool that school leaders can use to plan, navigate, and sustain reforms. The sustainability framework unveiled in the next section is used to benchmark the growth of reforms and is designed to help school leaders examine six sustainability factors of reform for meaningful, lasting school improvement.

Test Your Knowledge

We have learned that 3 decades of reform efforts have done little to narrow the student achievement gap—particularly for English learners.

1. Reflect on your education career. How many reforms have you seen come and go?
2. In your opinion, why do schools have difficulty sustaining reforms?
3. What are the consequences posed by this program-layering (reform after reform) effect?

INTRODUCTION TO THE SUSTAINABILITY FRAMEWORK

Thus far, this chapter has examined the navigation paths of school reform, a history of unsustained reforms through an examination of three major reform waves in this country, and has looked at the notion of reform distortion. It is now time to connect sustainability to school reform. Attempts to define the concept of sustainability are pervasive in the literature. Sustainability is more than a matter of persistence over time. It concerns more than the beginning and the end of a reform. Hargreaves and Fink (2000) explain that sustainability does not simply mean whether a reform can endure. The concept of sustainability addresses how initiatives can be developed without compromising the development of other reforms on site, both now and in the future. Century and Levy (2002) elaborate on the concept through an explication that sustainability is the capacity of a program to withstand shocks over time, to maintain core beliefs and values, and to use them to guide adaptation to change. What is clear to us is that the very essence of reform sustainability is characterized by complexity. This complexity calls for a multifaceted approach to the sustaining of reform efforts in public schools (Garcia, 2005).

Sustainability goes beyond the continuation of a reform. Perhaps part of the lack of success with reform sustainability is the way sustainability is viewed. There is a group of researchers offering a variety of perspectives for reframing reform sustainability in education. Goodman and Steckler (1989) describe sustainability structures along two dimensions: the breadth of the reform's integration and the depth of the initiative. Knight and Erlandson (2003) provide a framework for examining four factors that comprise educational reform: congruence, commitment, coherence, and continuity. Century and Levy (2004) offer a mathematical equation incorporating a multitude of variables to gauge sustainability. Examining the concept from a systems perspective, Fullan (2005) asks, how do you develop and sustain a greater number of systems thinkers in action? Drawing on corporate and environmental literature, Hargreaves and Fink (2006) profile seven sustainability principles. The reframing of reform sustainability calls into question an examination of the fundamentals that comprise this evasive concept.

Helping to unravel this complex web, Taylor (2006) points out that existing research has argued that sustainability is associated with an array of plausible variables (e.g., school capacity, political context, funding, alignment, leadership, faculty, retention, professional development, and so on) but has not yet proven consistent linkages between these variables and sustainability. One can conclude that a great deal is known about beginning new reform efforts, but little is understood about how to sustain them.

As shown earlier, reform in schools equates to change exacerbated by all its complexities. Ellsworth (2000) discloses that educators have made numerous efforts to design models or approaches that facilitate change in schools. These structural approaches are important because inevitably, individuals and organizations are compelled to change for a variety of reasons. However, no matter the reason, change is difficult. As a result, change needs to be carefully crafted as well as understood by all constituents.

The appeal for a sustainability tool has never been more apparent than in this current reform-driven era characterized by high-stakes testing and accountability. Christensen, Aaron, and Clark (2005) write that schools are incapable of reinventing themselves because they cannot create new capabilities and because school leaders do not have the tools they need to bring about change. If this is the case, then how can reform possibly be sustained and the achievement gap ultimately closed? Creating the kind of public education system that society demands requires an essential and systemic transformation with careful consideration to what fundamentally drives a reform and the subsequent application of these same traits to sustain it. The tool to help school leaders sustain reform efforts is found in the sustainability framework, defined by six prominent indicators that research shows not only drive reform but also sustain school reform. Table 2.1 profiles the sustainability framework with the indicators that, when carefully and methodically considered, can sustain reform efforts in schools—particularly those dealing with English learner populations.

In examining the sustainability framework, it is important to recognize that these indicators are linked by a pervasive influence: change—the necessary ingredient to carry out a reform. Change, and thus reform, appear to be primarily about recognizing and altering the interrelationships of these indicators. The indicators in the sustainability framework should be viewed as integrated and interrelated—they are critical to reform sustainability but not sufficient in isolation. The components are connected, impact one another, and infuse the entire framework. In its entirety, this reform tool can be used to identify patterns and trends in the deployment of a reform and subsequently allow leaders to make necessary adjustments to extend, accelerate, or terminate a given reform. The implications of this tool are far-reaching.

Each of the indicators in the sustainability framework is dissected and explained in detail in the core chapters that follow. The chapters will show how each of the indicators of the framework can be used to make reform work for school leaders instead of school leaders working for reform. The chapters will also demonstrate how the sustainability framework can easily be used to address the needs of English learners in schools and finally begin to close the achievement gap.

Table 2.1. Sustainability Framework

Indicator	Description	English Learner Reform	Leadership Implications
Instructional Leadership	From the district as well as the school levels, effective leadership that focuses on all students learning, inclusive of ELs, is at the core of educational reform. In this context, leadership is committed, persistent, proactive, and, most important, distributed through the school. Instructional leadership entails a focus on all students learning and is dynamic in that it connects and informs personnel, policy, programs, and practices in the school (Shannon & Bylsma, 2004).	Staff and all parts of the school organization are focused first and foremost on EL academic performance, with the leadership conveying the importance of the focus and taking action to implement strategies to improve learning (Shannon & Bylsma, 2004).	Leaders, focused and committed to addressing EL needs, realize there are "no quick fixes," and create a culture that encourages teachers to try new ideas and not to expect immediate results (Togneri & Anderson, 2003).
Alignment	Alignment in an educational system implies that all components are coordinated so that the system works toward a single goal: educating students to reach high academic standards (Hansche, 1998). In its simplest form, alignment refers to how well all elements in a school system work together to guide instruction and student learning (Long & Benson, 1998).	Alignment directly affects the degree to which valid and meaningful decisions about ELs can be made from assessment data (Long & Benson, 1998). The goal for schools that seek to narrow the EL achievement gap should be to increase alignment so that valid and effective data-driven decision-making can be accomplished (La Marca, Redfield, & Winter, 2000).	Leaders interested in closing the EL gap should be vigilant in alignment of content standards, performance standards, and assessments, whether assessment data are used to make policy decisions, funding allocations, or recommendations for student learning (La Marca et al., 2000).

Indicator	Description	English Learner Reform	Leadership Implications
Teacher Commitment	Teacher commitment to reforms to improve EL performance is crucial. The image of a committed teacher is one who: gives extra time, thought, and effort for students, school, and teaching; is willing to seek improvement, and to do things to an excellent standard; is engaged wholeheartedly, more than merely to fulfill responsibility; and has a vision and strives to do something right for the students (Choi & Tang, 2009).	Various factors have been found to enhance or diminish teacher commitment especially as it pertains to meeting EL challenges. In sustaining high levels of teacher commitment, researchers point out the importance of workplace factors such as: leadership, teacher autonomy, collaboration, feedback, learning opportunities, resources, and participation in decision-making (Leithwood, Jantzi, & Steinbach, 1999).	Teacher buy-in at the inception of a reform plays a critical role in the successful implementation of the reform. On the one hand, teachers who are happy with how the reform is working at their school, or whose ideologies match the reform, may be more likely to describe having participated in the reform adoption process in a positive way. On the other hand, teachers who are not in favor of the reform may be more likely to criticize or resist the adoption process, minimizing their role in it (Datnow, 2000).
Sustained Professional Development	Professional development has been described as a process of careful design. Some of the key components that have been highlighted in multiple studies include: engaging teachers in the context of their own classroom, strengthening content and pedagogical knowledge, providing opportunities for collaboration, and including experiences that engage teachers as learners (Johnson & Fargo, 2010).	Professional development in low-performing schools with ELs must address their work toward five interwoven areas: building on assets; challenging deeply held assumptions about students, staff, and learning; providing organizational memory for continuous improvement; focusing on instructional leadership routines; and integrating leadership development and organizational development within whole-school reform models that provide curriculum and instructional frameworks (Kruse, 2008).	Leaders should ensure that EL reform maintains an unyielding focus on learning. When learning is a primary focus of reform, it has the potential to permeate the school culture in ways that foster improvement (Kruse, 2008).

(continued)

Table 2.1. (continued)

Indicator	Description	English Learner Reform	Leadership Implications
Teacher Retention	Teacher retention is a problem in public schools that can and should be addressed if school reform is to be sustained. Nationally, 17% of the elementary and secondary teacher workforce leaves the public and private schools where they had been teaching every year. Although this turnover is inclusive of teachers transferring to another school, the implications of teacher retention on reform sustainability are enormous (Van Houtte, 2006).	EL reform poses the daunting task for teachers to focus on content mastery and English language development simultaneously. The top reasons for teachers leaving the profession were lack of professional support and poor school leadership (Carroll & Fulton, 2004).	The leader's role in retaining effective teachers in schools with large EL populations requires tending to a positive work environment that can lead to an increase in job satisfaction. An obvious reason for the interest in job satisfaction is its presumed relationship to job performance (Sweeney, 1982).
School Capacity	Cohen and Ball (1996) propose an expansive view of school capacity. In addition to teachers' knowledge and skill development, school capacity should encompass high-quality instructional materials and students and teachers who are motivated and ready to learn. Goertz, Floden, and O'Day (1995) describe dimensions of school capacity that include access to knowledge, school structure and resources, and leadership and norms.	EL reform requires a collaborative team approach: teams working together develop clear, operational understandings of their goals and strategies, fostering new ideas, skills, and a shared commitment to schoolwide improvement (Fullan, Bertani, & Quinn, 2004).	Studies support the now prevalent reform discourse suggesting that school capacity, which includes teachers' professional knowledge and skills, financial resources, and specifically effective leadership at the district and building levels, is important for increasing a school's ability for delivering high-quality instruction (Sipple & Killeen, 2004).

Chapter 2 Application Exercises:
Framing the Sustainability Framework in the Context of the English Learner Achievement Gap

Individual Exercise Schmoker (2006) argues that clarity precedes competence. As you begin to clarify the six indicators in the sustainability framework, how would you expand on the description/definition of each of these indicators? What behaviors would your school exhibit if each indicator was fully manifested? How can you as a leader take your school there?

Team Exercise At your next grade-level or department meeting, display a line graph that illustrates the English learner achievement gap. Ask your colleagues to identify the initiatives/reforms in the past 3 years that have focused on narrowing the gap. List these on chart paper. Distribute copies of the Reform Distortion Model. Ask team members to discuss ways in which reforms have been distorted at the different levels of the model and why. Reflect on approaches to eliminating barriers to reform implementation.

School Exercise Write one indicator from the sustainability framework on the top of six separate sheets of chart paper, numbering the pages one through six and posting them around the room. Count off by six into small groups, with each group moving to the indicator with the corresponding number to start the gallery walk. Ask groups to discuss ways in which the indicator is evident in your school and write one prominent example on the chart paper. After 4 minutes, have the groups rotate to the next chart paper and repeat the process. After completing the cycle, have one representative from each group report to the whole group.

3

The Loosely Linked Trinity

English Learner Identification, Program Placement, and Redesignation

The pursuit and promise of educational opportunity has historically been central in the path towards inclusion and a better life by groups in the United States who are struggling against forces of poverty, racism and prejudice. Now, protected by civil rights law, that promise is actually a pact. Schools have a legal responsibility to provide equal educational access and opportunity to all students—including language minority children who are not yet proficient in English (Olsen, 2010a).

One of the most challenging dilemmas facing school leaders undertaking English learner reform is the proper and coherent identification, placement, and redesignation of English learners in schools. What makes this a dilemma is the fact that unless this loosely linked trinity is tended to properly, this triangulation process can send an English learner into an educational abyss that exacerbates the achievement gap.

Schools tend to rely heavily on surrogate indicators such as home language surveys to identify English learners. If a language other than English is spoken at home as identified by the home language survey, the student is subsequently administered an English language proficiency test. However, language proficiency assessments used to identify and place English learners in programs are often flawed and fail to provide an accurate language profile of the abilities of the English learner. Short and Fitzsimmons (2007) caution that current identification measures do not provide the requisite information for accurate English learner identification and placement. There is a great deal of variation in the criteria that schools across the country use to identify students as English learners and in the proficiency tests used to help make decisions about placement. There is also much variation in the length of time it can take for an English learner to be classified as proficient in English or redesignated (Edvantia, 2007). As will be seen later in this chapter, some students carry the English learner label for the majority of their tenure in public schools. Astonishingly, some students graduate with the label of English learner even after having been in the same school district since kindergarten.

Having survived a less than authentic identification process, students in English learner programs are often placed in modified instruction, which translates to less linguistically and academically rigorous instruction than mainstream instruction. Callahan (2005) reminds us that in these displaced environments, English learners fail to acquire the grade-level academic and linguistic competency necessary to exit English development programs. This subtle, systematic tracking of English learners results in a lack of access to high-quality content-area instruction, which in turn has linguistic, academic, and programmatic consequences. Indeed, this lock-step accounts for the inability of English learners to catch up with their English-only counterparts. That there is a gap in educational achievement in the U.S. public school system is not news. That current English learner program practices in some schools may be contributing to the widening of the gap is becoming a revelation for many school leaders. The failing practices in schools, unfortunately, are not evenly distributed. They fall disproportionately on schools serving students identified as English learners.

From an organizational perspective, a less than authentic identification process, an uncertain placement policy, and a flawed redesignation process constitute hurdles that English learners encounter throughout their school careers through no fault of their own. Deep, schoolwide, structural reform is required in order to eliminate these organizational barriers for English learners. There is hope on the horizon for leaders interested in reform to address English learner needs. Under the auspices of instructional leadership, schools that are effective with English learner reform are characterized by distributed leadership. Guided by this type of leadership, Togneri and Anderson (2003) explain that distributed leadership is an essential component of building instructional capacity in a school. This concept is manifested when leadership is extended beyond the traditional positions of superintendent or principal to include teacher leaders, assistant principals, central office administrators, union leaders, school board members, and parents alike. Through distributed leadership, some schools have redefined leadership roles and have determined that no single stakeholder can tackle the complex challenge of instructional improvement alone—especially meeting the needs of the English learner population. In these schools, leadership is not simply shared; instead, stakeholders take on the elements of reform that they are best positioned to lead.

Through the methodical application of instructional leadership, a sustainability factor found to be central in school reform, this chapter argues for a school leader's attention to profound structural reform on how English learners enter, progress, and ultimately exit an English learner program. This deep reform approach is the epicenter for instituting sustainable school change to impact English learner achievement. Figure 3.1 depicts the trail of English learner identification, placement, and redesignation, serving as a backdrop for discussion on the essential work that leaders should undertake in order to bring about and sustain school improvement efforts for English learners. Indeed, this is where sustainable systemic reform has its inception. Integrating the sustainability indicator of instructional leadership, this chapter examines the crucial role that leadership plays as advocates for English learner school improvement efforts. In essence, Shannon and Bylsma (2004) write that these leaders ensure that staff and all parts of the school organization are focused first and foremost on English learner academic performance, with the leadership conveying the importance of the focus and taking action to implement strategies to improve learning. Specifically, this chapter addresses:

- The identification of English learners and levels of proficiency;
- The placement process and the importance of equal access to core curriculum;
- The redesignation of English learners and the unintended consequences of long-term English learners; and
- The role of instructional leadership in English learner reform.

This chapter provides the leader with a clear direction on how to bring about school reform for English learner success. Without a clear understanding of what constitutes an English learner program, Short and Fitzsimmons (2007) warn, school staff will have difficulty determining who these students are, how well they are doing academically, or what types of services they need.

ENGLISH LEARNER IDENTIFICATION

Wiley (1994) reports that in this country's public school system, three measures tend to be used most often to identify students as English learners: (1) self-reported information on the U.S. Census, (2) surrogate indicators (e.g., parents' replies to questions about their children on district- or state-developed home language surveys), and (3) language proficiency tests. Of the three, language proficiency tests offer the most consistent and common way to assign English learner status to students. In practice, school systems and researchers

Figure 3.1. The Process for Identifying, Placing, and Redesignating English Learners

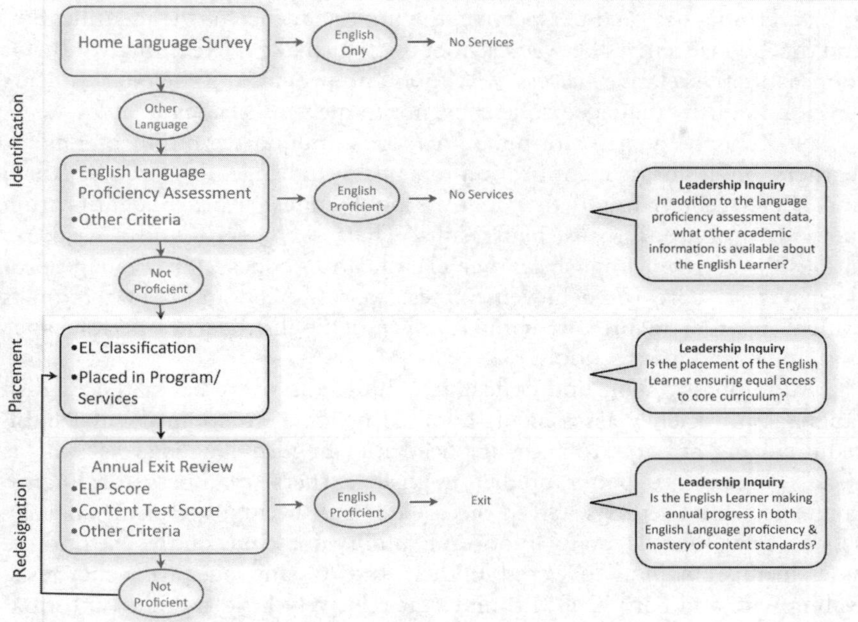

tend to rely heavily on these surrogate indicators to identify English learners. Based on the responses to the home language survey, a student may be identified as an English learner and then be tested for English language proficiency.

The validity of the identification process, however, is brought into question. August and Shanahan (2006) argue that current identification measures often do not provide the requisite information for accurate student placement. Issues such as age of enrollment in U.S. schools, educational background, and mobility all affect academic development, but are seldom elicited by home language surveys or language proficiency tests. Language proficiency tests share their limitations as well. Not only are they one-shot measures, but most districts do not include assessments in a student's home language. Additionally, Genesee, Lindholm-Leary, Saunders, and Christian (2006) say that measures of native language oral and literacy proficiency are strong indicators of English literacy development.

Adding to the complexity of the identification process, Batalova, Fix, and Murray (2005) found that school districts vary widely in their definitions of English learners. Some define these students as those who are eligible for language instruction services (e.g., ESL [English as a Second Language] classes), whereas others define them as those who are actually receiving such services. And as this chapter will show, schools differ in how they determine whether English learners should be exited from language instruction programs. From a national perspective, the impermanence of the identification and the inconsistencies between school districts make it exceedingly difficult to measure the relative success of schools and programs in helping students develop English language proficiency, not to mention academic literacy.

NCLB is helping to formulate a more common definition of English learners, but accurate identification remains a challenge. Research by Abedi and Dietel (2004) found that many school English learner identification methods produced inconsistent results. The researchers found a weak relationship between English learner classification codes and language proficiency test scores or achievement test scores. Accurate identification is critical in order to provide comparability of English learner performance both inter- and intra-schools.

Additionally, Wolf and colleagues (2008) discovered that the English language proficiency assessments adopted by states to comply with NCLB requirements attempt to measure academic English language as well as social language to better predict English learners' readiness for English language school settings. Given the use of English language proficiency assessments by schools, many important validity questions on the use of these assessments remain unanswered. In their study of language proficiency tests, Rabinowitz and Sato (2006) found that relatively little technical information from the test developers or states was available to indicate the technical quality of these assessments. The researchers proposed a comprehensive set of validation criteria to evaluate the technical adequacy of an English learner assessment system. Chapter 4 looks at assessment in English learner programs in more detail.

Understanding the levels of language proficiency is an important consideration for the reform-minded leader. Based on the results of an English language proficiency test, the student is given a language proficiency designation level. While English language proficiency tests and levels of proficiency vary across states, there are common characteristics of English learner levels of proficiencies. Differences are evident in the number of levels and descriptive terms used for levels. The number of levels of proficiency has ranged from three to six (Wolf et al., 2008). Table 3.1 outlines the overall descriptions used in California in English language development as an example. California includes five levels of English language proficiency and names the highest level "advanced." The descriptions under each level indicate differences in what English learners can produce. This matrix is an invaluable guide for school leaders in determining the proper placement of English learners into a variety of programs.

Table 3.1. The Five English Language Acquisition Levels: What English Learners Have (Comprehension) and Can Do (Production)

Level 1: Beginning
Students have: minimal comprehension and no verbal production *Students can:* nod answers to questions; move to show understanding; point to, categorize, match objects or pictures; draw *Classroom instruction should*: Incorporate "text to movement" (drama, Total Physical Response [TPR]) and "text to image" (drawing, graphic organizers) strategies to support English language comprehension and production Create a language-rich environment; provide listening opportunities with rich content Focus on highly contextualized activities to enable students to connect new information with primary language background knowledge
Level 2: Early Intermediate
Students have: limited comprehension and produce one-/two-word responses *Students can:* identify people, places, things, list and categorize; report memorable language; use everyday expressions independently *Classroom instruction should:* Incorporate "text to movement" (drama, TPR) and "text to image" (drawing, graphic organizers) strategies to support English language comprehension and production Ask yes/no and Who? What? Where? questions: have student complete sentences with one- or two-word responses; provide listening opportunities with rich content Focus on activities that enable students to derive meaning from key words and context clues
Level 3: Intermediate
Students have: good comprehension and enough proficiency to make simple sentences *Students can:* describe events, places, people, recall facts; explain academic concepts, define new vocabulary; retell information form text; summarize *Classroom instruction should*: Incorporate "text to image" (drawing, graphic organizers) and "text to speech" (oral language reprocessing/retelling) strategies to support comprehension and production of English language academic content Ask open-ended questions; model and expand student language; have students describe personal experiences Use collaborative "reading-into-writing" strategies (Language Experience Approach, Directed Reading-Thinking Activities) to develop content-area oral language and create authentic text

(continued)

Table 3.1. *(continued)*

Level 4: Early Advanced
Students have: excellent comprehension and make few grammatical errors *Students can:* give opinions; explain actions and views; negotiate with others; express the results of synthesis, analysis and evaluation *Classroom instruction should:* Incorporate "text to image" (drawing, graphic organizers), "text to speech" (oral language "reprocessing"/retelling) and "text to text" (written language) strategies to support comprehension and production of English language academic content Use collaborative "reading-into-writing" strategies (Language Experience Approach, Directed Reading-Thinking Activities) to develop content-area oral language and support reading and writing in different text genres and content areas Guide students in the use of reference materials with content-area text
Level 5: Advanced
Students have: near-native English speech *Students can:* produce oral and written language that is comparable to that of native English speakers at the same age *Classroom instruction should:* Incorporate "text to image" (drawing, graphic organizers), "text to speech" (oral language "reprocessing"/retelling), and "text to text" (written language) strategies to support comprehension and production of English language academic content Use collaborative "reading-to-writing" strategies (Language Experience Approach, Directed Reading-Thinking Activities) to strengthen content-area oral language and support reading and writing in different text genres and content areas Guide students in the use of reference materials with content-area text

Source: Santa Clara Unified School District, n.d.

Leadership Compass

Given the significance and the drawbacks associated with English learner identification, what role should the school leader play in ensuring that the English learner is given a fair chance in entering and subsequently succeeding in his or her school career? For starters, the instructional leader should engage in a regular and methodical investigation of the English learner identification process by ensuring that the English language proficiency assessment is properly used to determine the level of the students' English language proficiency. Additionally, Wolf et al. (2008) advise that other assessment data and teacher input adequately represent the students' knowledge and skills in the English language proficiency level and can be used as a basis to distinguish academic language attainment. If these checkpoints are not in place, then the instructional leader begins to reform the site so that this validation claim about English learner identification is firmly established.

The reform-conscious leader is reminded that the narrowing of the English learner achievement gap requires time and that the identification point for English learners is a good place to start. Shannon and Bylsma (2004) report that improved schools sustain engagement in educational reform over time. Organizational stability helps schools stay the course of school improvement, to persevere and persist. Change is seen as a long-term multistage process to attain high standards for all students. This school commitment to improvement efforts helps staff internalize the changes. As mentioned earlier, when well executed, instructional leadership can reap rewards in the form of sustained improvement over time.

From the district as well as the school levels, instructional leadership that focuses on all students learning, including English learners, is at the core of educational reform. In this context, Shannon and Bylsma (2004) argue that instructional leadership is characterized by committed, persistent, proactive, and, most important, as mentioned earlier, distributed through the school. Instructional leadership entails a focus on all students learning and being dynamic in that it connects and informs personnel, policy, programs, and practices in the school. Indeed, leaders have a critical role to play in the effective identification process of English learners by ensuring that the policies, procedures, and processes are giving English learners accurate and fair access to the curriculum.

Test Your Knowledge

Using the chart in Table 3.1, carefully examine the various levels of English learner proficiency. Identify the total number of English learners in your school and place the English learners in the levels accordingly. Now respond to the following questions:

1. Are your teachers aware of the English learner proficiency levels in their classroom?
2. How are the English language proficiency levels reflected in classroom instruction?
3. Can you and your teachers identify any English learners who may be placed in the wrong proficiency levels?

PLACEMENT

As noted in the previous section, English language proficiency tests are used to help identify English learners, determine their placement, and demonstrate their progress in attaining English. In researching English learner placement issues, August and Shanahan (2006) found four studies that examined whether a measure used for placement decisions was useful or appropriate, and none of these studies was of sufficient magnitude to allow decisive or comprehensive conclusions to be drawn. Although current language proficiency measures do not often provide the requisite information for accurate student placement, they are still the primary source in placing an English learner in English language development programs.

We have learned thus far that several problems and limitations have been associated with the use of English language proficiency tests for placement purposes. Most, for example, have not been good predictors of student success on reading and content-area assessments in English over time. Additionally, most of these tests do not supply teachers with information about a student's individual language strengths and weaknesses. August and Shanahan (2006) divulge that the state of assessments for oral proficiency and academic language lags behind literacy development assessments such as phonological awareness, word reading accuracy, and fluency. Genesee and colleagues (2006) found that problems associated with the identification of English learners include the lack of diagnostic assessments for reading comprehension and the lack of research to guide the placement and instruction of English learners with various types of learning disabilities. Chapter 7 addresses literacy issues facing English learners in more detail.

Because the language proficiency tests yield limited diagnostic information about the English learners' academic capabilities, English learner programs often place students in modified instruction, which translates to the diluting of academic content in mainstream instruction. Linquanti (2001) reveals that in these classes, English learners fail to acquire the grade-level academic and linguistic competency necessary to exit English learner programs. In essence, this constitutes nothing more than a built-in trap for the English learner. A study by Callahan (2005) looked at the effects of track placement of English learners to answer the question: Does track placement or English proficiency predict the academic achievement of English learners? Results indicated that track placement was a better predictor of English learners' academic performance than proficiency in English, highlighting the importance of quality instruction for English learners.

Track placement of English learners based on academic qualifications reflects what is called the principle of meritocratic selection (Dreeben, 2002; Mickelson, 2001). Dreeben (2002) asserts that as a strongly held American value, meritocratic selection requires basing judgments leading to selection or decisions on performance qualifications. The rationale for tracking assumes that instruction can be targeted more efficiently when classrooms are homogeneously grouped. Irrespective of whether homogeneous grouping works or not, tracking is widely practiced in the placement of English learners, and so how students get placed remains a subject of considerable interest and debate, especially when racial considerations are involved. Callahan (2005) insists that track placement requires that decisions allocating students to selective academic programs be based on evidence predicting successful achievement in these academic programs. In schools, students' current academic performance is generally considered the most relevant criterion for recommending or selecting students for courses that are differentiated by difficulty level. From the placement perspective, meritocratic selection puts the English learner at a distinct disadvantage at the onset.

At the elementary level, track placement takes the form of English language development instruction where English learners of similar language proficiency levels are grouped together and provided instruction to develop English language skills. Gándara, Rumberger, Maxwell-Jolly, and Callahan (2003) note that the common practice is to provide approximately 30 to 45 minutes of English language development daily. However, because English education must replace other instructional time, English learners receive less academic instruction time than their English-speaking peers. In secondary schools, English learners are often put in multiple periods of ESL classes instead of assigning them to full days in academic classes. Additionally, at the secondary level, Kelly (2007) points out that track placement is manifested when schools routinely offer courses with title modifiers such as honors, advanced, college prep, technical, business, or general. In investigating tracking, Hallinan (2004) found that about 80–85% of U.S. high schools have ability grouping at the course level and various loose forms of tracking.

For all practical purposes, this placement approach guarantees that English learners are more likely to attend classes and schools with other non-proficient, lower-achieving peers, which can hinder English learner progress. Validating this fact, Betts, Zau, and Rice (2003) argue that research supports the notion that the academic achievement of peers influences a student's own achievement.

The tracking of English learners begs the question of the confounding interaction between subject-area content and linguistic content. In other words, is the placement of English learners ensuring the attainment of academic content as well as the development of English language proficiency? Or, is tracking only widening the disparity between English learner and English-only academic performance? Wolf et al. (2008) recommend that continuous, on-site vigilance should be practiced to investigate the connection between the development of subject-area content and English language development.

Leadership Compass

Once the English learner is placed in a given program, then it becomes the instructional leader's moral as well as ethical responsibility to establish structures to monitor both the content knowledge progress and the English language proficiency attainment of the English learner. There is sound research advocating that content-area instruction can provide an excellent context for the development of academic English. Echevarria, Vogt, and Short (2004) argue that science, for example, involves the kind of learning through multiple modalities (speaking, reading, writing, doing firsthand investigations), which is often touted as characteristic of high-quality instruction for English language learners. In addition, attempts to teach academic language—the language of academic disciplines—separately from content-area instruction seems potentially ineffectual. Purcell-Gates, Duke, and Martineau (2007) reveal that students learn to read and write texts best by learning to do so in authentic contexts for authentic purposes.

From a school-reform perspective, Togneri and Anderson (2003) report that educational systems that showed improvement through successful reforms were committed to sustaining the reforms over the long haul. These schools set their courses and stayed with them for years. Additionally, longevity of leadership contributes to continuity and sustained improvement efforts. Snipes, Doolittle, and Herlihy (2002) point out that political and organizational stability over a prolonged period, along with consensus on educational reform, are preconditions for sustainable school reform. In essence, leaders, who are focused and committed to addressing English learner needs, realize that there are no quick fixes and create a culture that encourages teachers to try new ideas and not to expect immediate results (Togneri & Anderson, 2003).

Test Your Knowledge

Proper placement of English learners requires leaders to be vigilant as to how best to support students in programs. Adding to this complexity is the dual tasks that English learners face: the language demands of subject-matter instruction and the simultaneous development of English language proficiency. Reflecting on your school's English learner placement policies, respond to the following questions:

1. Are English learners given access to the same core curriculum available to your English-only students?
2. Is there evidence of tracking of English learners in your school?

3. Is content-area instruction being delayed for your English learners based on the assumption that English proficiency is a prerequisite for learning content?
4. How do your teachers reconcile English learner language development when contending with the language demands of subject-matter instruction?

REDESIGNATION

School leaders who are successful with English learner reform have instituted instructional supports that allow English learners to fully participate in content-area learning. In other words, the effective placement of English learners is at the forefront of the school improvement process. The third component of the loosely linked trinity is the redesignation of English learners. The term *redesignation* indicates the process by which English learners are determined to no longer need special language support services and/or are considered able to fully function in English-only classes. Some school districts use the term *reclassification*. A variety of sources are used by schools to determine whether English learners are ready to be redesignated. Jepsen and de Alth (2005) recount that these sources include state English language proficiency test scores, content test scores, school personnel (e.g., teacher, ELP specialist, or committee) input, parental or guardian input, student grades, portfolio assessments, interviews, and evaluations of classroom performance.

Good practice calls for English learner performance to be assessed regularly with the goal of redesignating the student. However, Jepsen and de Alth (2005) state that the current NCLB policy creates conflicting incentives that encourage increases in redesignation rates but also mandate high standards for English learner performance on standardized tests. Recent amendments to NCLB allow districts to include reclassified students (fluent English proficiency) with English learners in achievement score reports for up to 2 years. Researchers and practitioners alike argue that clustering redesignated English learners with current English learners provides the equivalent of smoke and mirrors by failing to provide a clear picture of English learner academic performance and thus not holding schools accountable for English learner results. Policies directed toward redesignation should attempt to resolve this discrepancy as well as consider whether English learners should be held to the same academic accountability standards as their English-speaking peers.

The redesignation of an English learner as proficient is the best measure of success for an English learner. The redesignation review from English learner to fluent English proficient status is a complicated process, however.

Lara (2001) reveals that while educational policies in some districts require only oral proficiency in English for redesignation, others require that students demonstrate academic proficiency through teacher grades and test scores. In California, for example, in addition to language proficiency, students must demonstrate academic proficiency through standardized achievement test results. The state's Board of Education suggests that districts use a combination of English proficiency scores from the California English Language Development Test (CELDT), academic achievement, teacher evaluation, and parental consultation. Parrish, Linquanti, Merickel, and Perez (2003) argue that in spite of this transparent direction, districts in the state have demonstrated great latitude in how they weigh these factors.

Moreover, these added mandates, Linquanti (2001) argues, have resulted in unintended programmatic consequences in that they have inadvertently created a class of English learners who are trapped in English learner programs. Long-term English learners are those who remain designated as limited English proficient after 5 or more years of enrollment in U.S. schools. The long-term English learner phenomenon is clearly evident in the state with the highest number of English learners in its public school system. In 2002 in California, according to Jepsen and de Alth (2005), schools on average reclassified 7% of their English learners. Of the English learners who achieved the board's recommended CELDT score, only 29% were redesignated, illustrating that the language proficiency test score is only one criterion used for reclassification. Years later, a 2009–2010 survey of 40 school districts throughout California found that 59% of secondary school English learners were made up of long-term English learners. This same study found that in one out of three districts, more than 75% of their English learners are long-term (Olsen, 2010b). More about long-term English learners is addressed later in this chapter.

The limited and sometimes conflicting research suggests that it can take English learners 6 to 10 years to be redesignated as proficient, while some English learners never achieve classification at the highest levels (Edvantia, 2007). A study that perhaps represents a best-case scenario was conducted in six Arizona schools. Researchers MacSwan and Pray (2005) examined the records of English learners who, on enrollment in the district (in grades K–3), had scored a 1 (no English) on the Bilingual Syntax Measure (the state-adopted language proficiency test), and who had been tested at least every 2 years. The children achieved a score of 5 or 6 (proficient) after a mean of 3.3 years. English (conversational) proficiency was achieved by about two-thirds of the children after 4 years and by more than 90% after 5 years. These three case scenarios illustrate the wide range in duration of redesignating a student once he or she has been classified as an English learner.

Beyond the state guidelines, adequate resources are important for the reclassification of English learners. Schools with large English learner populations must have the capacity to undertake the individual, comprehensive review process needed for redesignation. Additionally, Jepsen and de Alth (2005) advocate that English learners should have access to English learner–authorized teachers to prepare for reclassification.

Leadership Compass

The redesignation process requires the leader's vigilance if English learners are to break that structural trap common in many schools with high English learner populations. In addition to ensuring the annual measure of English language proficiency, it behooves the school leader to examine the alignment between the previous and current English language proficiency tests for every English learner. Wolf et al. (2008) write that these longitudinal analyses not only unveil potential growth patterns (or lack thereof) of English learners at the different levels of proficiency but also provide predictive power for English learner performance in content-area tests.

Olsen (2010b) advocates that the district has a critical role to play in English learner redesignation. It is the role of the district to ensure high-quality implementation of research-based programs for English learners through (1) clearly defined pathways and clear descriptions of program models in English learner master plans; (2) providing professional development (including coaching and collaborative time) for teachers and administrators in understanding the needs of English learners and strategies to meet those needs; (3) communication and clarity of expectations about what quality instruction looks like; (4) curriculum materials that facilitate differentiation for varying levels of English learner needs; (5) published expectations of growth and achievement for English learners by length of time in program and by proficiency levels; (6) systems of observation and mechanisms for monitoring student progress; (7) emphasis on articulation between levels; and, (8) systems for holding site administrators accountable for high-quality programs for English learners.

Togneri and Anderson (2003) remind leaders who are interested in English learner reform that schools driven by this type of leadership and committed to sustained improvement create a culture in which leaders encourage teachers to try new ideas and not expect immediate results. In these schools, teachers value consistency and focus, value initiatives that persist over time and that give them multiple opportunities to learn about changes they were expected to make. Additionally, Elmore and Burney (1997) assert that it is important for leaders to focus centrally on instructional improvement and to sustain that commitment long enough for people within the school to internalize it and to engage in problem-solving consistent with that commitment.

Test Your Knowledge

English proficiency is not in and of itself a guarantee of academic success for redesignated English learners. English learners must also achieve academic language skills and content-area knowledge and abilities before they can be considered adequately prepared to enter a mainstream classroom (Grissom, 2004). Within this context, respond to the following questions:

1. Are your English learners making progress in moving from one level of language proficiency to the next?
2. What is the redesignation rate for your English learners? From one school year to the next, what is the percentage of English learners reclassified as fluent English proficient (FEP)?
3. What are some of the factors preventing redesignation?

LONG-TERM ENGLISH LEARNERS

The introductory segment of this chapter alluded to the concept of the loosely linked trinity (identification, program placement, and redesignation) as requiring deep structural reform by leaders in order to narrow the achievement gap. Schools that have not addressed this trinity have found themselves with an ever-increasing, disproportionate population of English learners along with a lagging redesignation of English learners. Olsen (2010b) says that the existence of long-term English learners is evidence that for many students, the school experience that should have propelled them toward English proficiency and academic success has indeed been an educational dead-end.

Chapter 1 described the three cohorts of English learners that traditionally populate schools in the United States. Of the three cohorts, the long-term English learner poses some of the greatest challenges to educational leaders. Faltis and Wolfe (1999) report that long-term English learners schooled primarily in the United States are generally orally proficient but have poor reading and writing skills and little control of academic English. Many long-term English learners, Linquanti (2001) argues, are unable to exit from English language development programs because their academic achievement is not at grade level. As explained earlier, placement in low-track classes, according to Callahan (2005), contributes to the perception of English learners as limited in language, limited in knowledge, limited in skills, and limited in cultural competencies.

So who are these long-term English learners? Olson (2010) asserts that to a large degree, educational policy, program development, curriculum resources, and professional development have sought to address this issue by focusing on English learners in the elementary school grades. The assumption had been that by the time English learners get to secondary school, they would already have developed the skills to participate on an equal footing with English-proficient students—and that English learners who are enrolled in middle and high school are more newly arrived immigrants. Surprisingly, the vast majority of English learners currently in middle schools and high schools have been enrolled in U.S. schools since kindergarten—and most were born in the United States. This group is struggling academically, failing to progress in English proficiency, and facing disproportionately high dropout rates.

School districts across the United States are facing the challenge of how to serve long-term English learners. A 2009 report by the Colorado Department of Education examined English learner data by number of years in U.S. schools. The study concluded that there is no clear, easy reason revealed by data to explain why students are remaining in the English learner category for 10+ years. Similarly, a national study conducted by the Council of Great City Schools of English learner programs in five school districts concluded that while districts were unanimous in voicing their concern for long-term English learners, finding effective interventions to move these long-term students along the proficiency continuum remains a challenge (The Council of Great City Schools, 2009).

The phenomenon of long-term English learners is not new. What is striking, Olson (2010) asserts, is that these students have remained unaddressed in a time of intense accountability and major initiatives that purportedly were designed to meet their needs. In the past decade, school districts across the nation have set in motion major reforms intended to address the underachievement of students and close the achievement gap. It was assumed that these reform initiatives would meet the needs of English learners along with other students. The achievement gap between English learners and proficient English speakers actually widened in the past decade.

School leaders befuddled by the widening gap are beginning to realize that there are English learners in their schools who, despite having initially entered U.S. schools in the primary grades, are now stalled in their progress toward English and struggling academically. These long-term English learners, Olson (2010) explains, carry labels such as "ESL Lifers," "The

1.5 generation," "Forever LEP," and "The 6 Plusers." These long-term English learners make up the "English learner Ghetto"—a concept to be addressed in detail in Chapter 5.

SUSTAINABILITY INDICATOR: INSTRUCTIONAL LEADERSHIP

This chapter has focused on demystifying the English learner trinity—that triad process of identification, program placement, and redesignation of English learners that, when not tended to by leaders, results in an increase in long-term English learners. This chapter has also argued for the reform-conscious leader to take a bold stand and address the flaws that are now clearly evident in this complex triad. As mentioned earlier, the hallmark indicator of the sustainability framework is the role that instructional leadership plays in successful implementation of English learner school reform. From the district as well as the school level, effective instructional leadership that focuses on all students learning, and in this case English learners, is at the core of educational reform. In this context, Shannon and Bylsma (2004) emphasize that leadership is committed, persistent, proactive, and, most important, distributed through the school. Instructional leadership entails a focus on all students learning and is dynamic in that it connects and informs personnel, policy, programs, and practices in the school. Staff and all parts of the school organization are focused first and foremost on student learning, with the leadership conveying the importance of the focus on English learners and taking action to implement strategies to improve learning for this population of students. In other words, this sustainability indicator ensures that schools are programming for students first and adults second, and not the reverse. School improvement takes time, and the reform strategies must be sustained by educational leaders for significant change to occur.

School reform leaders who are serious about addressing the prevalent achievement gap between the English learners and the English speakers in their schools have a variety of avenues available to them. Knapp and colleagues (2003), for instance, suggest that leaders persistently and publicly focus their attention and that of others on learning and teaching. They identify essential tasks for instructional leaders such as:

1. Making learning central to their own work—in the case of English learners, ensuring that student placement is creating the effects intended to create.
2. Consistently communicating the centrality of student learning—for English learners, the leader insists on the continuous examination of student data reflecting progress in English language proficiency as well as academic content.

3. Articulating core values that support a focus on powerful, equitable learning—for English learners, ensuring that meritocratic selection or tracking is not impeding English learner progress.

This chapter has highlighted the loosely linked trinity of English learner identification, program placement, and redesignation as the primary driver requiring the school leader's attention in order to narrow the achievement gap. This chapter has also explored the concept of long-term English learners and culminated by spotlighting the benchmark indicator of the sustainability framework: instructional leadership. A well-grounded instructional leader uses the concepts addressed in this chapter to create cognitive dissonance in staff by continuously examining the English learner progress in his or her site.

The rubric provided in Table 3.2 is provided as a tool for school leaders to dialogue with staff on your school's progress in English learner programming.

Chapter 3 Application Exercises:
Unwrapping the Loosely Linked Trinity of English Learner Identification, Program Placement, and Redesignation

Individual Exercise Using Table 3.1, or your own matrix, chart the progress of English learners by proficiency levels. What factors are keeping your English learners from moving from one proficiency level to the next? What additional resources or attention is required for English learners to achieve proficiency?

Team Exercise At your next school leadership team meeting, list your grade levels vertically on chart paper and then draw five columns reflecting number of years horizontally (i.e., 1, 2, 3, 4, 5+). Now identify the number of English learners under each column by grade level. Analyze your chart by discussing the number of long-term English learners in your school. Discuss factors that have aided or hindered English learners' advancement toward English proficiency.

School Exercise Count off by threes into small groups, ensuring a mixture of people who do not see each other on a daily basis. Have the small groups reflect on the principle of "meritocratic selection" and have each group respond to the following questions: Where and how are English learners placed based on their English language proficiency levels? Are content areas being deferred as a result of the placement? Is there evidence of subtle tracking of English learners in our school? Host a whole group debriefing by focusing on the implications of the small-group discussions.

Table 3.2. English Learner Identification, Program Placement, and Redesignation Rubric

Element of English Learner Programming	Emerging Stage	Developing Stage	Sustainability Stage
Identification of English Learners	The identification of English learners is based primarily on state-required language proficiency test with no assessment in the student's home language. This process is carried out by designated staff with no teacher participation in the process.	In addition to state criteria, the identification of English learners includes measures of native language proficiency. Teachers are minimally involved in the identification of English learners.	Native language proficiency, as well as literacy proficiency measures, are used in addition to state-required language proficiency tests to identify English learners. Teachers are not only involved in the identification process but their input adequately represents the student's knowledge and skills in the language proficiency level.
Placement of English Learners	The placement of English learners is based solely on the student's performance on the language proficiency test with no consideration of other factors such as educational background or mobility. English learners of similar language proficiency levels are grouped together and provided instruction in English language skills. Teachers have minimal knowledge of the language proficiency levels of their students.	In addition to language proficiency test performance, English learner placement considers native language proficiency and literacy proficiency. English learner instructional placement reflects multiple language proficiency levels and provides instruction in English language skills. Teachers have knowledge of the language proficiency levels of their students and adjust their instruction accordingly.	English learners are placed in research-based programs with clearly defined accelerated pathways ensuring the rapid acquisition of English language proficiency and the attainment of academic content. English learners are mainstreamed with English-only peers and are regularly monitored. Teachers are well versed in the language proficiency levels of their students and modify instruction accordingly.
Redesignation of English Learners	The redesignation of English learners is based solely on performance on language proficiency results. The redesignation of English learners is at a low rate.	In addition to the English learner performance on language proficiency tests, students demonstrate academic proficiency through teacher grades and standardized test scores. The redesignation of English learners is at a medium rate.	There is a system to regularly assess English learner performance. Parental consultation, teacher evaluation, and academic achievement are considered in addition to the student's performance on language proficiency tests. The redesignation of English learners is at a high rate.

4

The Fallacy Behind English Learner Assessment

The Elephant in the Room

> *If we are finally to connect assessment to school improvement in meaningful ways, we must come to see assessment through new eyes. Our failure to find a potent connection has resulted in a deep and intensifying crisis in assessment in American education. . . . Our current assessment systems are harming huge numbers of students for reasons that few understand. And that harm arises directly from our failure to balance our use of standardized tests . . . in the service of school improvement. When it comes to assessment, we have been trying to find answers to the wrong questions. (Stiggins, 2002, p. 1)*

The barriers to reframing assessment policy and practices in public education are formidable. When it comes to standardized tests, Americans have a prideful bond with standardized tests. Berlak (2001) says that tests used for making school improvement decisions have a profound hold on U.S. society because Americans comprise a culture where numbers depicting performance help compare and rank the order of individuals and institutions. Educators and the public alike readily operate under the assumption that test scores provide valid information about children and their preparation to perform academically. As products of this society, Americans have come to accept standardized tests as a measure of children's intellectual and academic capacities and abilities. Americans cannot fathom a public education system devoid of standardized tests.

The executive summary of National Literacy Panel on Language-Minority Children and Youth (August & Shanahan, 2006) reported that adequate assessments are essential for gauging the individual strengths and weaknesses of English learners, making placement decisions, and tailoring instruction to meet student needs. Concomitantly, the panel's report unveiled a stunning admittance: that existing assessments are inadequate to the needs of English learners. Most assessments, the panel found, do not predict how well English learners will perform over time on content-area assessments in English. If the institutional gauge to measure English learner academic progress is flawed, what is the reform-minded leader to do in navigating the school improvement process to impact English learners? This revelation poses leadership implications of how current assessments are used to identify, to place, to monitor, and ultimately to redesignate the English learner.

Considering that the majority of states use their language proficiency tests as a primary source to identify English learners, to determine their level of proficiency, to place them, to monitor their progress, and ultimately to redesignate their English learner status, Wolf et al. (2008) argue for taking note of the issue of comparability of these assessment results. Figure 4.1 illustrates the reverberations of assessments policies in English learner programming. As this chapter will show, these English learner assessments are an ethical and a strategic blunder. They constitute an ethical blunder in that they misguide educators with invalid information from which potent English learner decisions are made. They are a strategic blunder in that they serve to exacerbate the English learner achievement gap.

Figure 4.1. The Complex Amalgam of English Learner Assessments

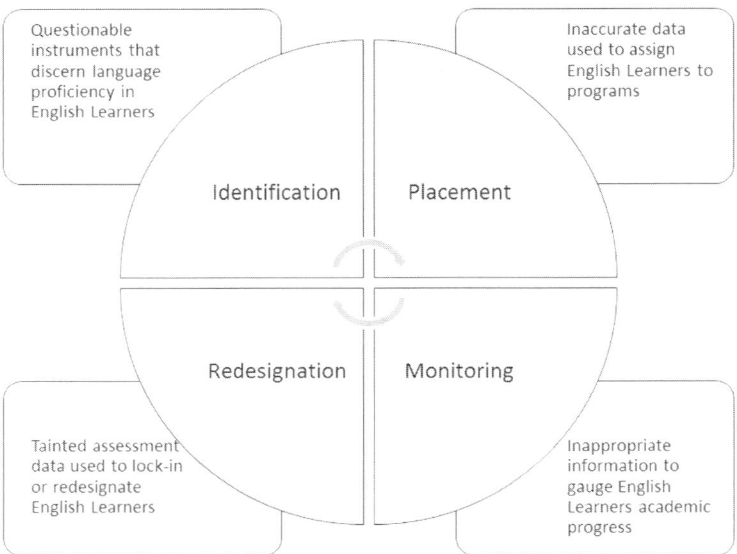

It is the decision of the actual placement of an English learner in the classroom that launches him or her into a journey of uncertainty and ambiguity. Pemberton, Rademacher, Tyler-Wood, and Perez-Cereijo (2006) write that without solid, effective assessments, even experienced teachers can be hard-pressed to disentangle students' difficulties in learning English from issues related to their educational background and native language literacy skills. Miramontes (1987) notes the difficulty in distinguishing normal English acquisition from academic delay and/or learning disabilities without culturally and linguistically sensitive assessments. Compounding this argument, Echevarria and Graves (2003) assert that standardized tests that aim to measure academic language (e.g., math, science, literacy) are not sensitive to second language literacy development. What is perceived as lack of mastery of the content by English learners, Solano-Flores and Trumbull (2003) argue, is often instead the normal pace of the second language acquisition process. These tests are influenced by English learners' complex factors, such as native language literacy, family background, educational history, mobility patterns, and that they often make reference to cultural experiences or historical background to which many English learners have not yet been exposed (Pemberton et al., 2006).

This flawed system of English learner assessment has ripple effects. These consequences, Artiles and Ortiz (2002) point out, manifest in an increasing number of districts exhibiting patterns of either over-representation or underrepresentation of English learners in special programs. Considering the significant role that an effective assessment system plays in guiding decisions about schools and students, it is of paramount importance to ensure that a legitimate assessment system is in place as a school begins the journey of English learner reform.

Under NCLB (No Child Left Behind), states, districts, and schools are required to demonstrate that English learners are making progress not only in meeting academic standards but also in becoming fully proficient in English. Both types of progress, as Chapter 7 will show, depend on effective literacy development. However, effectively assessing this dual progress is an insurmountable task for the school leader. In the broadest sense, assessments provide information about the extent of standards or content attainment that in turn influences classroom practice. In education circles, this concept is referred to as alignment. The technical quality of both standards and assessment undoubtedly affects the quality and degree of alignment. The fundamental purpose of an assessment system, La Marca, Redfield, and Winter (2000) argue, is to determine the degree of alignment necessary to make just decisions regarding classroom practice. The focus of this chapter, therefore, is to enhance school leaders' understanding of issues surrounding English learner assessment as well as to offer reform insights so that sustainable narrowing of the achievement gap becomes a reality. The sustainability factor of alignment is dovetailed in this chapter to make transparent the relationship between assessment and the continuous improvement of classroom practice.

This chapter examines:

- Language proficiency assessment;
- Standardized assessment of academic language;
- Assessment and the school improvement process; and
- Alignment as a sustainability indicator.

LANGUAGE PROFICIENCY ASSESSMENT

Whether the assessment of language development versus the content attainment argument is driven by a philosophical bend or a political stance, the issue is relevant to both sides. As Chapter 3 demonstrated, language proficiency assessment plays a critical role at the onset of an English learner's academic career. What remains ambiguous is the relationship between language proficiency development and content attainment and how to systematically assess these two dynamics. Wolf et al. (2008) argue for further study in the confounding connection between subject-area content and English language development.

Two studies have identified a correlation between English language proficiency and content-area achievement on large-scale academic assessments. Oakeley and Urrabazo (2001) found that in Texas, English learners' level of English proficiency on the Woodcock-Muñoz Language Survey was found to be highly correlated with their scores on statewide assessments of reading, math, and writing. In a similar study, Mahon (2006) found parallel results in Colorado in a study of 200 4th- and 5th-grade English learners in four elementary schools.

Contrasting these findings, however, researchers at the National Center for Research on Evaluation, Standards, and Student Testing found a weak relationship between English learner classification codes and English learner scores on both language proficiency tests and achievement tests (Abedi & Dietel, 2004). To what extent linguistic knowledge influences English learners' performance both on content and English language proficiency assessments remains uncertain. What is certain, however, is that these tests do not gauge what they intend to measure. Thus, the scores do not tell teachers or policymakers what they need to know about students' content knowledge and, in fact, may be misinterpreted (Short & Fitzsimmons, 2007).

It should be noted that the responsibility for the development of valid English learner assessments falls on the state and not the school districts. In an effort to strengthen the assessment connection between English language development and content attainment, many states have begun to develop their English language proficiency (ELP) standards with an emphasis on academic language. However, an examination of the states' ELP standards and the constructs defined in the assessments reveals varying degrees of specifying the nature of academic English proficiency. The extent to which these various new language proficiency assessments accurately measure academic language remains uncertain, and hence, poses a validity concern. Another notable issue is the mismatch in proficiency levels established in the standards and those used in the ELP assessments. While states are establishing the technical adequacy of the use of their new ELP assessments, issues of comparability and alignment in the constructs also need to be addressed in their validation arguments (Wolf et al., 2008).

The revised language proficiency assessments are beginning to make efforts to measure academic language as well as social language to better predict English learners' readiness for English language school settings. However, many important validity questions on the use of these assessments remain unanswered (Wolf et al., 2008). In their review of language proficiency assessments, Rabinowitz and Sato (2006) found that relatively little technical information from the test developers or states was available to analyze the technical quality of these assessments. The researchers proposed a comprehensive set of validation criteria to evaluate the technical adequacy of English learner assessment systems. Similarly, Wolf et al. (2008) reviewed the current literature and policy regarding English learner assessment in order to inform practitioners of the key issues to consider in their validation process. The areas reviewed include the procedures of English learner identification and redesignation, the characteristics of English language proficiency assessments, including validity information, and the use of accommodations in the assessment of content knowledge. All this to say that the school leader should be cognizant of the fact that batteries to assess language proficiency in English learners are a work in progress and require further development to get them to a point where instructional decisions about English learners can be made with sound confidence. In the interim, the leader is to carefully scrutinize the data extrapolated from these instruments as well as the use of said data to make English learner decisions.

Leadership Compass

There is little argument that assessment policy in education in the United States is influenced by federal dollars. Wolf et al. (2008) assert that the No Child Left Behind (NCLB) legislation has had a great impact on states' policies in assessing English learners. The legislation requires states to develop or adopt sound assessments that validly measure English language proficiency, as well as content knowledge and skills in English learners. However, while states have moved rapidly to meet these requirements, they face challenges to validate their current assessment systems for English learners, partly due to the lack of resources.

It is these two requirements of gauging English language proficiency and content knowledge attainment simultaneously with valid assessment instruments that pose challenges for the reform-minded school leader. The role of the leader attempting to narrow the English learner achievement gap is to reconcile the validity issue of English learner assessments while simultaneously ensuring that the complex amalgam is working toward enabling and not stalling English learner reform.

A school leader interested in validating the uses and inferences made from assessment results should be aware that this process involves producing diverse sources of evidence as well as inferences made based on an assessment. Wolf et al. (2008) argue that it is not the test itself that is validated; rather, validation applies to specific interpretations and uses intended by a particular test. Tests themselves are not valid or invalid, the researchers explain; instead, validation is the accumulation of evidence by which particular interpretations or uses of tests are justified. According to the Standards for Educational and Psychological Testing, validity evidence can be obtained by examining the content of the assessment (usually referred to as content validity), the interrelationships between the assessment and other measures (criterion-related validity), the internal structure of the assessment (construct validity), and the test takers' response processes. Additionally, test fairness or bias is an important component of validity, particularly for English learners, who are a culturally and linguistically diverse group.

The complex role of assessment has long intrigued researchers and practitioners alike. The issues of test validity are paramount to the school leader who is interested in reforming a school to better address English learner academic results. As Stiggins (2002) puts it:

> We are a nation obsessed with the belief that the path to school improvement is paved with better, more frequent, and more intense standardized testing. The problem is that such tests, ostensibly developed to "leave no student behind," are in fact causing major segments of our student population to be left behind because the tests cause many to give up in hopelessness—just the opposite effect from that which [is] intended. (p. 3)

The practicality of this discussion resides in the sheer awareness that language proficiency assessments, as they currently stand, have their limitations and it therefore behooves the school leader to be sensitive to how the information gleaned from these assessments is used to make decisions about English learner identification, placement, monitoring, and ultimately, redesignation. In essence, the school leader is tasked with legitimizing English learner assessments so that English learners have access to core curriculum and are not being sent off into an educational abyss where the very system that is trying to educate them is in actuality suppressing their academic growth. To put it differently, Stiggins (2002) offers profound questions for reflection: How can the positive impact of the assessment scores on learners be maximized? How can we be sure that assessment instruments, procedures, and scores serve to help learners want to learn and feel able to learn? It is the school leader's responsibility to mitigate invalid assessments with informative assessments.

Test Your Knowledge

English learners have the dual challenge of attaining academic content while developing English language proficiency. Having accurate assessment data ensures appropriate instruction and support for the English learner.

1. At what intervals are the English learners in your school assessed, i.e., quarterly, each semester, and so forth?
2. In addition to the English language proficiency test, what diagnostic assessments help determine English learners' strengths, weaknesses, knowledge, and skills?
3. How are formative assessments used to provide ongoing information concerning English learner progress?

STANDARDIZED ASSESSMENT OF ACADEMIC LANGUAGE

At the close of the 20th century, Haertel (1999) asserted that the power of high-stakes testing to influence classroom instruction had been oversold. It is worth noting that the important debate on the role of assessment as a catalyst for reform is not assisted by the exclusive identification of assessment with testing. There is little or no argument that standardized tests, as they are administered by public schools in this country, aim to measure academic knowledge. In theory, standards-based assessments are aligned with the standards and the core curriculum, and provide detailed feedback to teachers and students about student skill levels in relation to standards. In practice, however, this configuration is far from coherent.

Wolf et al. (2008) reviewed practices on the inclusion of English learners in testing for Adequate Yearly Progress (AYP) reporting. The study found that all states had adopted NCLB's mandate for including all English learners in the statewide assessments regardless of English proficiency levels. The researchers also found that new Title I regulations allow states to exempt newly arrived English learners (students who have attended schools in the United States for 12 months or less) from AYP calculations. Recently arrived English learners are allowed to be exempt from assessments in reading/English language arts but are required to be included in mathematics assessment (which does not have to be given in English). In accordance with this regulation, many states follow the exemption for recently arrived English learners, and some allowable variations pertaining to the reading/English language arts exemption were observed in the study. While states and school districts are addressing the policy of English learner inclusion in standardized testing of content attainment, the argument about how to measure academic language attainment intensifies.

Having navigated through a questionable language proficiency assessment, the English learner finds him- or herself in a program facing the tough challenge of learning English while attempting to master content, or what some education circles refer to as academic language. There is a lack of consensus from the research community as well as the practitioner landscape on what exactly is meant by the academic language that standardized assessments are purported to measure. Herein lies a definitional quagmire. In attempting to define academic language, some researchers focus on linguistic features (e.g., grammar, lexis), and others highlight cognitive aspects and contextual features (e.g., strategy use, schemata/background experiences, higher-order thinking, metalinguistic awareness) (Wolf et al., 2008). For discussion purposes, academic language is used synonymously with academic vocabulary due to the strong relationship between vocabulary knowledge and academic achievement (Marzano, 2004). The lack of a common framework to describe academic language poses a challenge to school leaders who are attempting to operationalize the constructs into their standards and assessments. Bailey (2007) argues that a movement to develop a practical framework of academic English for school settings has recently arisen to encompass various aspects of academic language. Such a model is proposed in Chapter 9.

The standardized assessment of academic language is further exacerbated by the limited vocabularies of English learners. August, Carlo, Dressler, and Snow (2005) write that English learners are especially likely to have underdeveloped English vocabularies. Additionally, Umbel, Pearson, Fernandez, and Oller (1992) argue that this barrier is even evident in English learners who come from middle-income backgrounds. Adding to this discourse, Capps et al. (2005) assert that the largest and fastest-growing populations of English learners in the United States are students who immigrated before kindergarten and the U.S.-born children of immigrants.

The conundrum, however, lies in the fact that, as Scarcella (2003) argues, this population enrolls in U.S. schools at kindergarten; by middle school, few of these learners need instruction in basic English, yet many lack the academic language central to text comprehension and school success. Recall that this student cohort was classified as long-term English learners in Chapter 3.

The sparse background of academic language in English learners raises a profound question: Is not standardized assessment in U.S. public schools missing the mark when it is testing something that English learners do not possess? This equates to nothing more than testing children on material that has not been previously taught. So how limited is this academic language in English learners? For starters, Swanson, Saez, and Gerber (2006) found that with English learners in the elementary and middle school years—whether formally designated as limited English proficient or not—these students' vocabulary levels were well below average. The issue may be more widespread than an English learner issue. Lesaux, Kieffer, Faller, and Kelley (2010) suggest that many struggling readers in mainstream classrooms— whether they are English learners or not—lack the specialized academic language needed for school success.

This section has demonstrated that the academic language that standardized testing is aimed at assessing is lacking in English learners. Year after year, English learners are placed in a self-defeating dilemma of taking standardized assessments in which they are unable to demonstrate mastery. Is it fair, then, to assess English learners on something that they may be lacking? Doesn't this incoherent, if not unethical, testing policy serve simply to exacerbate the English learner achievement gap?

Leadership Compass

As required by law, all states now implement standardized, standards-based tests in reading/English language arts and mathematics for grades 3 to 8, plus at least one high school grade level. Additionally, most states also have now begun to assess science. As shown earlier, under NCLB, English learners must be included in these standardized assessments and must be provided appropriate accommodations in order to accurately measure their content knowledge (Wolf et al., 2008).

Wolf et al. (2008) researched the states' allowances of accommodations for English learners in standardized testing. Decisions on which accommodations English learners are allowed to use were often part of a school- or district-level decision-making process. The researchers found that 23 states specified a school-level process, and 11 states specified a district-level process. Six states designated local teams or committees to make the determinations; however, it was unclear whether these local teams were at the school or district level. Furthermore, even if a state policy mandated district-level decision-making, that did not preclude the district from then delegating the decision-making process to each school. At the time of their study, the remaining 10 states had no publicly available information about who was delegated to make decisions regarding accommodations for English learners.

Wolf and colleagues (2008) further found that many states mentioned multiple criteria in determining which accommodations were allowed for English learners on state academic assessments. For example, 29 states mentioned that accommodations should be made on an individual basis, and 22 states said that the accommodations used during testing had to be the same accommodations as those used during classroom instruction and assessment. Other selection criteria required by some states were English proficiency level of the student (as determined by the state-approved ELP assessment) and number of years a student has been in school and designated as an English learner. Additionally, some states required documentation of allowed accommodations to be placed in the English learner's file.

To make assessment of English learner progress as valid, and hence, as legitimate as possible for English learners—that is, to have instruments that measure what they profess to measure—the reform-minded leader has at his or her disposal the use of accommodations in the assessment of academic language. These accommodations may come in the form of safety nets (Supovitz & Poglinco, 2001) that are structured into the school day and year and that provide students with extensive support and multiple opportunities to achieve the standards.

Test Your Knowledge

NCLB provides latitude in English learner assessment in the form of accommodations. These accommodations, when used properly by the school leader, help legitimize assessments for English learners. Based on this assumption, respond to the following questions:

1. What forms of assessment accommodations does your school provide for English learners?
2. Are these accommodations effective in yielding additional English learner assessment data?
3. How do you reconcile the accommodations with the standardized assessments in your English learner placement decisions?

ASSESSMENT AND THE SCHOOL IMPROVEMENT PROCESS

One of the most incompatible features of accountability systems (including NCLB) in public education is that these structures assume that student academic progress (when depicted on a line graph) follows a straight, upward trajectory. In other words, school improvement efforts based on the results of standards-based tests are expected to reflect growth and improvement unabatedly. While in theory this assumption may hold, in practice it does not. Because learning is not linear, this assumption is quickly invalidated when one reaches a school's doorsteps.

A report by Massachusetts education leaders on trends in schools making Adequate Yearly Progress under NCLB reflected a profound and realistic statement: "At some point, test scores plateau. . . . Straight line projections may look nice, but they do not occur in real life" (MassPartners for Public Schools, 2005, p. 1). A vast doubt is cast on the ability of schools to meet ever-increasing performance targets, such as the targets for percentages of students scoring proficient under NCLB in the context of the plateau effect. The Center on Education Policy (2009b) found that under test-based accountability systems, initial gains in test results observed during the first few years are inflated and difficult to sustain, and education leaders should therefore expect to see student test results level off over time. This realization poses potent implications for the reform-minded leader, not only in how to measure progress in school reform but also in how to sustain teacher morale when the plateau effect becomes evident.

In their study of improvement trends in low-performing schools, Elmore and City (2007) found that there are no breakthroughs or dramatic turnarounds in the schools' improvement. The researchers discovered that there are predictable periods of significant improvement, followed by periods of relative stasis or decline, followed again by periods of improvement. The researchers termed this phenomenon as the plateau effect. These erratic patterns of student performance are common in the school improvement process. To think otherwise is unrealistic at least and delusional at best. Even the private sector is defined by performances that ebb and flow with the tide of time.

Additionally, Elmore and City (2007) argue that periods of flat performance in the school improvement process raise some of the most difficult challenges that leaders face—particularly those leaders who are focused on sustainable school improvement. It is disheartening for schools, the researchers write, where everyone is working hard by incorporating new practices into their work with students, when planning and collegial activities move adults outside their comfort zone, and yet the school sees no visible payoff. Figure 4.2 illustrates Elmore's (2005) perception of the reality of the school improvement process juxtaposed with the linear expectation of NCLB.

Figure 4.2. The Reality of School Improvement

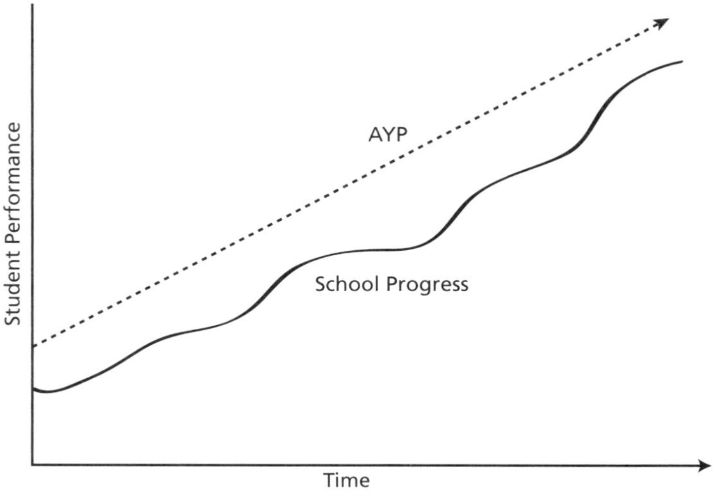

Source: R. F. Elmore (2005).

Elmore and City (2007) observed several practices in schools that thrive in spite of the plateau stages: (1) They anticipate the flat periods and persist through them; (2) they have a theory about how what they are doing will result in improved student performance; (3) they develop finer-grained measures for detecting improvement; and (4) they make adjustments when evidence suggests that their efforts really are not working.

Offering a counterpoint and helping to further conceptualize the flat periods in school improvement, the Center on Education Policy (2009a) examined the dynamics of the plateau effect using a database of test results in reading and mathematics from all 50 states. The center analyzed 55 trend lines from 16 states showing the percentages of students scoring at the proficient level on state tests between 1999 and 2008. This study only included states with at least 6 years' worth of data to ensure that trend lines were long enough to allow time for a plateau to emerge. The results of the center's study were insightful. Only 15 of the 55 trend lines in the data set exhibited a plateau pattern. Instead, percentage proficient trend lines followed a wide variety of patterns, and the only predictable pattern was an overall upward trajectory. The study also unearthed 21 instances of steady increases in test scores over time, and 19 instances where the percentage proficient zigzagged up and down unpredictably. All but one trend line had an overall increase.

This study also revealed periods of student academic improvement emerging between the first and second years of testing and between the third and fourth years. Additionally, the researchers identified increases when higher-stakes policies were added to existing state accountability systems, as was the case between 2003 and 2004, the first 2 full years of testing after NCLB was enacted. The center's researchers concluded that the plateau effect should not be assumed in the current accountability context.

The patterns revealed by this study pose two implications. First, it is possible (and common) to see large gains using a test that has been in place for a long period. Second, raising the stakes attached to test results can lead to a substantial increase in performance, even on tests that have already been in place for 4 or 5 years.

Test Your Knowledge

When plotted on a line graph, English learner academic performance will vary from school to school—even among schools reflecting similar student demographics. Whether or not you subscribe to the concept of the plateau effect as a normal phase of the school improvement process, reflect and respond to the following questions:

1. Over a 3- to 4-year span, what does your English learner performance look like on a line graph?
2. Is there evidence of the plateau effect and/or increases in your English learner performance?
3. What variables may have contributed to the plateau effect and/or increases in English learner performance?

SUSTAINABILITY INDICATOR: ALIGNMENT

The second indicator in the sustainability framework is alignment. Without question, alignment is a significant differentiator in school reform. Much of the literature on systemic reform uses the terms *fit*, *alignment*, and *coherence* to denote the need for all aspects of an educational system to be coordinated in unison. Hansche (1998) explains that alignment in an educational system implies that all components are coordinated so that the system works toward a single goal: educating students to reach high academic standards. In other words, alignment refers to how well all elements in a school system work together to guide instruction and student learning.

Long and Benson (1998) assert that alignment directly affects the degree to which valid and meaningful decisions about student learning can be made from assessment data. Alignment in educational systems is a dynamic and cyclical process. This cycle requires the school leader to be vigilant as English learner academic achievement information migrates through the various stages. La Marca et al. (2000) note that, at a fundamental level, the goal for school reform should be to increase alignment so that valid and effective data-driven decision-making can be accomplished.

Systems alignment, and the alignment of standards with assessments in particular, is a vibrant process. Standards provide a framework from which to develop assessments, which in turn provide information regarding the attainment of standards. Assessment results provide the opportunity for data-driven decision-making. The decisions made may involve instructional or curricular change. Assessment data may also affect a decision to modify expectations for student knowledge and skill development. In short, alignment can improve teaching and learning relative to standards (Long & Benson, 1998). In their study of the role of alignment in English learner systemic reform, Garcia, Cesario, Stanga, and Mangewala (2010) found that alignment is a precursor to the sustainability of English learner systemic school reform. In other words, English learner systemic school reform has little chance of success, much less sustainability, in the absence of alignment. As shown in Figure 4.3, the reform-conscious leader should focus on maintaining an alignment between standards, assessment, and classroom practices. In its simplest form, this alignment refers to how well the three elements in a school system work together to guide reform.

Figure 4.3. School Alignment Cycle

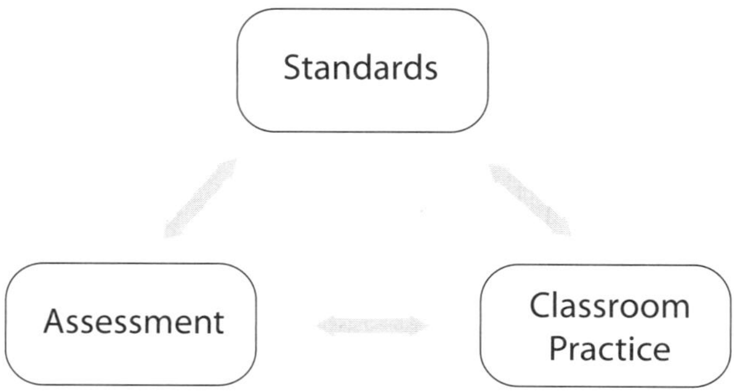

Calling for practical features of alignment in schools, Supovitz and Poglinco (2001) advocate for the careful attention to: (1) a common core curriculum that is aligned with state standards; (2) standards-based assessments that are aligned with the standards and the core curriculum, and that provide detailed feedback to teachers and students about student skill levels in relation to standards; (3) distributed school leadership structure, led by the school's leader, that coordinates implementation, analyzes results and sets performance targets, ensures the necessary resources, and aligns schedules and other school activities with implementation of the design; and (4) safety nets that are structured into the school day and year and that provide students with extensive support and multiple opportunities to achieve the standards.

The inference can now be made that the English learner assessment link in this alignment cycle is deficient. Previous sections showed that language proficiency tests lack the validity from which meaningful decisions can be made about English learner identification, placement, monitoring, and redesignation. Standardized tests used to measure academic language are not designed to factor in language proficiency development in English learners. In his call for balanced assessments in education, Stiggins (2002) argues for a different approach in which assessment can contribute to school improvement efforts that are largely ignored by the current accountability movement. He contends that if assessments of learning (standardized assessments) provide evidence of achievement for public reporting, then assessment for learning (formative assessments) can serve to help students learn more.

For the purposes of discussion here, the concept of alignment is denoted as a call for the instructional leader to advocate for informative assessments to supplement, not supplant, the bureaucratic-mandated batteries that serve only to lock the English learner into insurmountable academic paths. Barnes, Clarke, and Stephens (2000) make two fundamental observations regarding the function of assessments: Attempts at school reform are likely to be futile unless they are accompanied by matching assessment reform; and assessment can be the engine of reform, or the principal impediment to its implementation. The implementation of any reform agenda in education will be severely hampered by any lack of credibility in either the content of the proposed curriculum, or the means by which its outcomes will be assessed.

For many years, researchers pointed to a lack of alignment of curriculum, standards, and assessment as a cause of the failure to change teachers' practice and bring about effective school reform. Embedded in this argument is the notion that poor alignment results in teachers having difficulty interpreting and acting upon the policymakers' demands (Penuel, Fishman, Gallagher, Korbak, & Lopez-Prado, 2009).

In bringing closure to this segment, there is one other point to be addressed. Tending to the alignment at the school site is half of the job for the reform-minded school leader. The other half involves tending to the district demands. Chrispeels, Burke, Johnson, and Daly (2009) point out that the most common element of misalignment in school systems is the disconnect between the district and the schools. Although a district and its schools may share a common focus on improving achievement, they frequently hold different views about how this is accomplished. Thus, a critical tension exists between the school and district in maintaining the balance between school autonomy and district coherence and control. Although this tension is likely to always be present, district office staff and school teams may benefit from more clearly articulating a theory of action regarding leadership teams and their role in the improvement process (Agullard, Huebner, Goughnour, & Calisi-Corbett, 2005).

Argyris (1993) writes that this reality indicates a need to explore ways in which school leadership teams might serve as a wider bridge between schools and the central office in the reform process. The potential of school leadership teams, further explored by Talley and Keedy (2006), indicates that effective teams actively engage in making curricula and instructional decisions to facilitate bottom-up problem-solving.

This chapter has profiled the paramount and questionable role that language proficiency tests play in English learner programming. It has also discerned how standardized tests are not designed to measure English language development in English learners. Additionally, the chapter has described the plateau effect as a feature in school improvement efforts. And lastly, the chapter examined how ensuring the alignment of classroom practice to assessments and to standards is nonnegotiable for the reform-minded leader. Having provided a sound conceptual understanding of assessment in English learners programs here, the next chapter features the leader's charge in structuring flexible program options for English learners.

The rubric shown in Table 4.1 is provided as a tool for school leaders to dialogue with staff on the school's progress in English learner programming.

Table 4.1. The Effective Use of Assessments in English Learner Reform

Element of English Learner Programming	Emerging Stage	Developing Stage	Sustainability Stage
Standardized Assessment of Academic Language	A process to use assessment results for the improvement of EL performance is lacking. There is no examination of assessment results to discern whether ELs are mastering academic language. The importance of mastering academic language in the classroom is not addressed.	Staff analyzes EL results from high-stakes state and local assessments with a focus on academic language attainment. Findings are shared with grade levels and/or departments and teachers are expected to review the results and address areas in need of attention. Periodic discussions on how to improve EL programs ensue.	Using a collaborative approach, teams of teachers utilize the cycle of inquiry process as an ongoing analysis of EL performance on academic language. EL assessment results are discussed regularly and used to identify strengths and weaknesses in classroom practice. EL performance in both formative and summative assessments is used to promote program improvement for ELs.
Assessment and the School Improvement Process	There is no systematic process for using EL assessment results for school improvement purposes. The monitoring of EL achievement is left up to individual teachers.	Assessment results are used to identify ELs in need of additional support for learning. ELs needing help are provided minimal interventions with the hope that their academic performance will improve. The achievement gap between English learners and English-only students persists.	A coherent and coordinated intervention program is in place for ELs who persistently need support based on assessment results. Individual ELs are monitored using both formative and summative assessment results. A multilevel support system ensures that ELs are succeeding academically. Assessment results reflect a narrowing of the EL achievement gap.
Alignment	There is no effort to align standards, assessments, and classroom practice. State and local assessments are administered to ELs but minimal attention is paid to the results. Teachers profess to be addressing standards but there is little evidence in EL test results.	Periodic discussions ensue among teachers on their use of EL assessment results to align their classroom practice with state/local standards. There is minimal commitment to the role that EL assessment plays in aligning/adjusting classroom teaching.	Collaborative teams of teachers work to use EL assessment results to inform, improve, and align their individual and collective practice. There is a regular and dedicated time for school teams to discuss EL academic performance with a focus on aligning classroom practice to standards.

Chapter 4 Application Exercises:
Addressing the Fallacy Behind English Learner Assessments

Individual Exercise Develop a strategy for ensuring that appropriate accommodations are provided in the standardized assessment for English learners. Your strategy should reflect the expectation that the accommodations used during testing are the same accommodations as those used during classroom instruction. How would you begin hosting conversations with your staff about these accommodations? How do you plan to articulate the outcome of your strategy?

Team Exercise At your next school leadership team meeting, distribute copies of the Amalgam of English Learner Assessments (Figure 4.1). Carefully examine the four dimensions on the graphic, paying close attention to the role that assessment plays in each of the dimensions. Host a dialogue with your leadership team about the ripple effects of the flawed system of EL assessment. How are these questionable assessment processes contributing to the EL achievement gap? What implications do these policies pose for classroom practice?

School Exercise At your next staff meeting, establish groups of three to five of job-alike teachers. DuFour, DuFour, Eaker, and Many (2006) assert that teacher dialogue moves from sharing opinions to building shared knowledge of best practice through collective examination of assessment results. Have the groups reflect on the following questions: How often does your team review samples of EL student work? How are the EL challenges with academic language manifested in these reviews? How does the team adjust instruction based on the examination of EL student work? Allow opportunity for whole-group debriefing.

5

Flexible Program Options

The Pathway out of the EL Ghetto

> *English learners experience U.S. schools and schooling differently than their native English-speaking counterparts. English learning educators often focus on teaching English to the extent that entry into content-area academics is delayed until enough English has been acquired. As a result, English learners often find themselves on the periphery, physically and pedagogically outside of the richest academic discourse. (Callahan, 2005, p. 309)*

The schooling environment for English learners, according to Harklau (1994), is substandard, limited to low-level, remedial coursework that is meant to compensate for students' limited language skills. In the peripheries of mainstream classrooms, Valenzuela (1999) asserts, English learners have little chance to interact in English with English-dominant students. In these environments, teachers' expectations are low, and negative student–teacher relationships prevail. The road to school failure has already been established; not only do English learners struggle to cross linguistic and academic boundaries, but they must also contend with their physical positioning outside of the mainstream. More often than not, English learner classrooms are located on the periphery of, if not outside, the main school building.

Callahan (2005) argues that the logic behind exposing English learners to a less challenging curriculum resides in educators' misconceptions about linguistic as well as academic abilities. Principals, teachers, and counselors interpret limited English proficiency as a form of limited intelligence and place students in low-track classes to compensate for this perceived deficiency. Katz (1999) found that track placement limits access to academic and linguistic content and influences teachers' beliefs about and treatment of students. The researcher contends that teachers' low expectations of English learners results in perpetrating institutionalized racism against the

English learner population. Substantiating this argument, Valenzuela (1999) warns that when they are placed in low-track classes, English learners find that teachers expect little of them academically, and when little is expected, little is produced. Hence, a vicious journey begins toward failure for English learners in U.S. schools. There is little doubt that English learner placement in the peripherals of the school process serves to further exacerbate the academic achievement gap. It is no wonder that despite decades of school reform efforts, the English leaner achievement gap remains prevalent to this day. In organizational behavioral theory, this is a classic example of addressing the symptom of the problem rather than the cause.

School leaders' and teachers' misconceptions of English learners represent just the tip of the iceberg. The fragmented and rigid structure of schools is the subtle enemy of English learners and resides well below the surface of the water, making it almost impossible to detect its sheer magnitude. Olsen (2010a) insists that the fragmented programming experienced by English learners is a result of contrasting school decisions and perspectives from one classroom teacher to another, and from grade level to grade level regarding how the needs of English learners should be addressed within a school. At the elementary level, for example, because a student may have been in a primary language preschool, then in an English-only classroom for kindergarten with no English Language Development (ELD), followed by a year in a classroom with a teacher who emphasizes strong ELD, then the student may receive no services for a year, and then be back in a bilingual program. A long-term substitute teacher placed in a bilingual classroom may not believe in the program, and may emphasize English—while the preceding teacher may have emphasized the home language and done little (Valdés, 2001). As if the incoherent programming were not bad enough, entry into the secondary schools, in departmental classrooms, is where the English learner begins to head toward the abyss. Figure 5.1 illustrates the fragmented and incoherent programming that English learners experience, through no fault of their own, and yet it is a structural school dynamic to which most educators are oblivious.

Valdés (2001) says that inconsistencies in the fragmented and rigid schooling for English learners result from multiple factors: lack of clear district language policy and guidelines defining what should be occurring, leaders who lack understanding about what should be in place, inadequate professional development for teachers, and the lack of effective ELD materials so that what gets used in one classroom may or may not bear any resemblance to what gets used in another. However it happens, the lack of consistent language development in English and in their home language that occurs in the lives of English learners leaves significant gaps—linguistic and academic. This bouncing from one program to another or the alternating

Figure 5.1. The Incoherent Schooling of English Learners

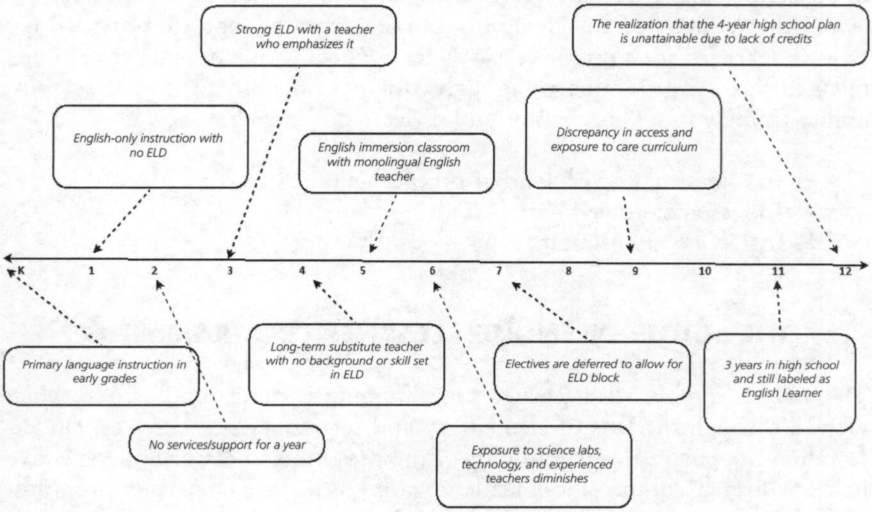

placement of an English learner program one year and mainstream another is what Olsen (2010a) refers to as the Ping Pong effect. The researcher notes that the research on language and academic progress makes clear that consistency and flexibility in English learner programs matter across the grades, as does faithful implementation of research-based models and teacher commitment. The coherence and flexibility of a program over time are major factors in producing high achievement for English learners. Yet English learners enjoy very little of this.

The strongest testament for advocating for flexible yet effective programming for English learners resides in the stunning phenomenon of long-term English learners in public schools today. Scarcella (1996) reveals that, as they are academically unprepared to participate in a rigorous high school curriculum, these long-term English learners are caught in a cycle of under-preparation. During elementary school, they focus on acquiring the English necessary to survive in an English-only classroom, while their native-English-speaking peers develop math, science, and literacy skills. The sobering truth of the failure of English-only programs to meet the academic needs of English learners resides in the fact that 94% of long-term English learners participate in an English-only curriculum for 70% or more of their elementary school years. By the time they reach high school age, these students are behind academically and lack the skills necessary to exit English learner programs.

With this context in mind, this chapter advocates for the reexamining of the school structure for English learners. This chapter makes clear for the leader that coherence and flexibility in the programs that are provided for English learners are a dire necessity. The important role of teacher commitment in flexible programs is highlighted as a critical factor in the sustainability framework. This chapter addresses the following:

- The status of English learner programming;
- The issue of equity; and
- Lost in the mainstream.

THE STATUS OF ENGLISH LEARNER PROGRAMMING

The structure of English learner programming is better understood when viewed through the lens of elementary and secondary perspectives. Understanding the purpose and emphasis of the programs under each perspective helps to strengthen the school leader awareness of English learner programming from a systemic point of view.

Elementary Models

Although they may vary from school to school, there are three common models of English learner programs in elementary schools: Structured English Immersion, bilingual education programs, and Two-Way (or dual-language) programs. Olsen (2010a) emphasizes that mainstream placement is not a model at all for English learners, though in reality, many English learners find themselves in this type of abyss. The models differ in the languages used for instruction, goals, student grouping, and outcomes. Historically, there has been controversy about which of the three listed above is more effective and about the role that primary language instruction plays in producing positive English learner outcomes. Long-term outcomes looking at both the strength of English literacy and at academic success have affirmed that the simultaneous development of both English and the home language facilitates higher outcomes in English literacy, and also provides more access and fewer gaps in academic content (Menken & Kleyn, 2010). Figure 5.2 illustrates the three English learner models common in elementary schools.

Structured English Immersion. Structured English Immersion is a program that is overwhelmingly in English and one in which teachers attempt to make subject matter comprehensible for the English learner. In an English Immersion program, Foorman and Carlson (2006) explain that teachers

Figure 5.2. English Learner Models in Elementary Schools

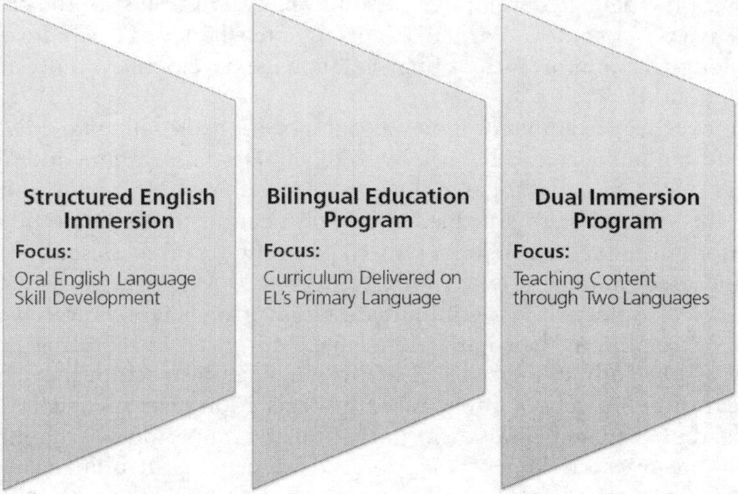

of English learners face other challenges as well in trying to plan for and provide instruction that addresses oral language skills in English. Teachers in English immersion programs face the challenges of balancing English literacy instruction. To at least some degree, the former is dependent on the latter. Thus, as will be shown later, English language development itself simply cannot be supplanted with literacy development.

The challenges of this program, however, are notable. In their evaluation of Structured English Immersion programs in the Los Angeles Unified School District, Hayes and Salazar (2001) found that class size and the delivery of Structured English Immersion had created a number of difficulties for English learner educators. The researchers concluded that few English language development lessons and experiential hands-on learning activities were provided. The researchers additionally found little evidence of primary language support. In their study, most classrooms were devoid of primary language materials or any materials reflecting the children's ethnic or cultural heritage. When evidence of primary language was observed, it was only in the form of books. Many teachers in English Immersion programs relied on paraeducators for language clarification with students. Classroom discourse was conducted largely in English and the primary language was used principally with children entering with low ELD levels. Overall, teachers agreed that everything needed to be taught at a much slower pace with much repetition. Teachers tended to rely on oral instruction in this English learner model.

Bilingual Education. In the case of bilingual programs, teachers face the formidable task of balancing primary language literacy instruction and English oral language development. Additionally, with most of the curriculum delivered in students' primary language, teachers can easily lose sight of the long-term importance of English language development (Foorman & Carlson, 2006).

An excellent example of issues and implications in bilingual education can be found in the research work by Mitchell, Destino, Karam, and Colon-Muniz (1999), who investigated the impact of California's Proposition 227, where the state's voters amended their constitution to eliminate bilingual education. In outlawing bilingual instruction, the researchers said, this referendum used political power to resolve technical arguments over whether students who enter school with limited English proficiency can receive continued instruction in their native language. Moreover, in requiring English learners to be fully immersed in English language instruction during their first year of public school attendance, this legislation places language learning ahead of academic attainment during this initial period of schooling.

Despite research evidence supporting the benefits of bilingual education programs, there are still technical questions about bilingual education as a language development program. There is, according to Mitchell et al. (1999), a great deal of confusion in distinguishing the politics from the process of nurturing linguistic and academic success. Language learning in the public schools must be fully understood politically if it is also to be understood educationally and linguistically. All this is to say that the controversy behind bilingual education appears to be motivated more by politics rather than by learning. Longitudinal studies examining the effectiveness of bilingual education are still in the works.

Dual Immersion Program. Dual Immersion programs, also known as Two-Way Immersion, is an increasingly popular hybrid of bilingual education in the United States in which English-speaking children and minority language speakers learn together in the same classroom, with the three goals of bilingualism/biliteracy, cross-cultural understanding, and high academic achievement for all (Gomez, Freeman, & Freeman, 2005).

In Dual Immersion programs, Palmer (2007) contends that teachers teach both languages through content according to preset program design decisions. While there are a wide variety of Dual Immersion programs, the two most popular program models are known as the balanced or 50:50 model, in which instruction for all grade levels is balanced evenly between the two languages; and the "minority language dominant" or 90:10 model, in which instruction begins in kindergarten with 90% of the day in the minority language and 10% in English, and English instruction gradually increases each year until by the 4th or 5th grade, the percentages are equal. Interestingly, the majority of Dual Immersion programs in the United States involve Spanish as the minority language.

The controversy behind this program resides in its questionable impact on English learners. Palmer (2007) claims that because of the English-only school that surrounds this program, in a sense boxing it in on all sides, there is significant deficit framing of language minority students at the school, and their language and culture go underappreciated. While students are to some extent protected by their teachers and offered tools for facing the larger world, the context in which the program is administered cannot be ignored.

Palmer (2007) concludes that a Dual Immersion program in the public school system in this country, whether it is a strand program or a schoolwide program, is always operating within an English-dominant environment and therefore has a responsibility to work on both fronts: Teachers must attempt to offer children alternative discourses and an opportunity to develop strong academically oriented identities, while simultaneously working to educate and collaborate with colleagues, community members, and the larger society to counter any dominant discourses that may be working to negate their efforts.

In summary, the three types of elementary programs for English learners, while having the common goal of English language attainment, are lacking in their ability to fine-tune that balance between English language development and content attainment.

Secondary Models

In the secondary schools, the daunting task for English learners is the racing of the clock. Short and Fitzsimmons (2007) maintain that one of the most significant challenges for schools that serve adolescent English learners is helping them become proficient in English and meet high school graduation requirements in the designated timeframe. Implementing the best program to do so is a difficult proposition given the diversity among the learners in terms of their backgrounds and aspirations and the policies in place that conflict with what is known about the second language acquisition process. Compounding this program rigidity dilemma is the fact that English learners comprise a transitional group. In other words, as English learners are becoming proficient in English and are redesignated, a new set of English learners is constantly coming into the fold.

Callahan (2005) notes that the United States' public education system continues to favor the traditional 4-year high school model for all, even though adolescent English learners as well as some native-English-speaking students might be more successful with a 5- or 6-year option. This inflexible system allocates course credits based on seat time, and in some cases end-of-course test scores, rather than other means for demonstrating competence in a subject. Additionally, receiving a diploma in many states requires passing a standardized exit exam.

Educators are in denial mode, thinking that English language acquisition can be readily developed in the timeframe offered in secondary schools. Collier (1987) warns that it is a myth that adolescent English learners can learn the academic English they need for schooling in 1 or 2 years of specialized instruction. The researcher maintains that most English learners require 4 to 7 years of instruction to reach the average academic performance of native English speakers, so time is of the essence for those who enter high school as beginning English learners. Compounding the language acquisition issue, Graves (2006) cautions that the academic vocabulary challenge alone is overwhelming. High school students, according to the researcher, are expected to have a vocabulary of approximately 50,000 words to be able to master the increasingly complex coursework of high school, and the average student learns 3,000 new words each year. In 4 years, then, the average beginning English learner might learn 12,000 to 15,000 words without targeted interventions, falling far short of the 50,000-word goal. When they have to perform double the work, learning academic English while learning the content of multiple subjects, they are at a decided disadvantage in the country's schools.

The racing of the clock for secondary English learners, coupled with the challenge of learning English while attempting to master content, is further exacerbated by our national accountability system. NCLB defines high school graduation rates in a particular way: Only students who receive a regular, standards-based diploma, on time with their class, are to be counted as high school graduates. Many secondary English learners enter 9th grade with limited English skills and fragmented educational backgrounds and therefore need additional time to graduate. Thus, this NCLB accountability measure is a significant challenge to students and schools (Short & Fitzsimmons, 2007). Table 5.1 illustrates the pathways available to English learners at the high school level. The framework noticeably illustrates the narrowing and the deferring of the curriculum in doubling up on the ELD component.

In summary, the effectiveness of English language development, at both the elementary and secondary levels, continues to be the cause of much debate among researchers and practitioners alike. There is no empirical evidence to suggest whether a separate ELD block is necessary and/or sufficient for teaching and learning English if English language development is effectively taken care of in the content area classroom. In the context of English Immersion programs, wherein virtually all instruction is delivered in

English, one might question whether a separate oral ELD block is necessary because students are immersed in English throughout the day. In the context of bilingual programs, at least at the early grades, where literacy and content-area instruction are delivered in the primary language, one might question whether a separate block of 30–45 minutes is sufficient for introducing students to English (Foorman & Carlson, 2006).

Regardless of which English learner model is in question, the common denominator is the ELD component. In other words, the goal of all English learner programs is to help the English learner acquire English language proficiency so as to function successfully in the mainstream classroom. In reality, however, there is widespread poor implementation across models in the K–12 environment. In practice, ELD in many classrooms and across program models has tended to be weak. The development of home language literacy and language has often been weak as well. The result has been that many English learners do not develop strength in either language (Olsen, 2010b).

Leadership Compass

As highlighted in the previous section, the fundamental goal of an English learner program is to develop English language skills in the English learner so that language ceases to be a learning barrier in the mainstream classroom. Whether programming at the elementary or secondary levels, the leader's focus should be on the continuous monitoring of and evaluation of the effectiveness of the ELD component of the English learner program in their schools. It is in the leveraging of the ELD feature of any program that will help realize the fundamental goal of an English learner program.

It merits recalling that Menken and Kleyn (2010) found that the ELD pullout model or ELD as the only component of the school day designed to address English learner needs has been found to produce weak outcomes over time, and does not sufficiently address a major goal of schooling, which is access to and mastery of academic subjects. Although English learners in these settings may appear to be progressing adequately in English in the primary grades, as they continue on to upper elementary grades and secondary schools where language demands increase significantly, they fall further and further behind.

Most secondary school English learner programs are designed with newcomers in mind. The ELD classes are designed as a 3- or 4-year sequence, and students are placed in them by English proficiency level as determined by their scores on the language proficiency test. In California, English learner Specially Designed Academic Content in English (SDAIE) content classes are the placement

Table 5.1. Pathways Available to English Learners at the High School Level

	LEP 1/2	LEP 2/3	LEP 3	LEP 3/4	LEP 4/5	5/RFEP*	RFEP
9th	ELD	ELD	SDAIE** English	SDAIE English	9th English	9th English	9th English
	ELD	ELD	ELD				
	ELD	EL Earth Science	SDAIE Earth Science	Earth Science/ Biology	Earth Science/ Biology	Earth Science/ Biology	Earth Science/ Biology
	Algebra Readiness/ Algebra 1	Algebra Readiness/ Algebra 1	Algebra/ Geometry	Algebra/ Geometry	Algebra/ Geometry	Algebra/ Geometry	Algebra/ Geometry
	PE	PE	PE	PE	PE	PE	PE
	Elective/ Foreign Lang	Elective/ Foreign Lang	Elective/ Foreign Lang	Elective/ Foreign Lang	Elective/ Foreign Lang	Elective/ Foreign Lang	Elective/ Foreign Lang
	Algebra Readiness/ ELD	Algebra Readiness/ ELD	ELD				

	LEP 1/2	LEP 2/3	LEP 3	LEP 3/4	LEP 4/5	5/RFEP*	RFEP
10th	ELD	ELD	SDAIE English	SDAIE English	10th English	10th English	10th English
	EL World History	EL World History	SDAIE World History	SDAIE World History	World History	World History	World History
	EL Biology	EL Biology	AE Biology	Biology	Biology	Biology	Biology
	Algebra Readiness/ Algebra 1	Algebra/ Geometry	Geometry	Geometry			
	PE	PE	PE	PE	PE	PE	PE
	ELD	Elective	Elective				
	ELD	ELD	ELD				
11th	ELD	ELD	SDAIE English	SDAIE English	11th English	11th English	11th English
	EL U.S. History	EL U.S. History	AE U.S. History	AE U.S. History	U.S. History	U.S. History	U.S. History
	EL Earth Science	EL Earth Science	AE Earth Science				
	Algebra	Geometry	Geometry/ Algebra 2	Geometry/ Algebra 2			
	PE/Health	PE/Health	PE/Health	PE/Health	PE/Health	PE/Health	PE/Health
	ELD	ELD	Elective				
	ELD	ELD	ELD				

(continued)

Table 5.1. *(continued)*

	LEP 1/2	LEP 2/3	LEP 3	LEP 3/4	LEP 4/5	5/RFEP*	RFEP
12th	ELD	ELD	SDAIE 12th English	SDAIE 12th English	12th English	12th English	12th English
	ELD	ELD	SDAIE Civics/ Economics	AE Civics/ Economics	Civics/ Economics	Civics/ Economics	Civics/ Economics
	ELD	EL Biology					
	Algebra	Geometry	Algebra 2	Algebra 2			
	Elective	Elective	Elective	Elective	Elective	Elective	Elective
	ELD	ELD					
	ELD	ELD					

* Reclassified Fluent English Proficient

** Specially Designed Academic Instruction in English

Source: English Learner Master Plan, Santa Clara Unified School District.

for English learners until they get through an intermediate level of proficiency. For long-term English learners, who seem to plateau at an intermediate level of proficiency, districts and schools using this approach to placement keep long-term English learners in these separate English learner settings indefinitely. For example, if a long-term English learner remains at a CELDT Level III (see Table 3.1) for 3 or more years, they remain in the ELD III class. Because they remain in these classes for years, this becomes in many ways an "ESL ghetto," according to Valdés (2001). Research from New York City indicates that this is the pattern for most long-term English learners, though it appears to be less prevalent in California. Eight of the 40 districts that responded to the Californians Together survey indicated that this is the approach in their schools. Long-term English learners, based on their CELDT level, are put in the same classes with other English learners (Olsen, 2010b).

Finding an effective ELD program is not an easy task. Gersten and Baker (2000) note that at the elementary level, teachers readily admit to having considerable confusion and uncertainty about the focus and content of language development instruction. Teachers often ask whether such instruction should involve primarily directed lessons and exercises and/or more naturalistic, conversational activities. Should it concentrate on language objectives and/or content-area objectives? Should such instruction focus on communicative skills and/or more academic uses of language? All these fundamental, if not philosophical, questions are reflective inquiries that school leaders should be asking of staff.

In this context, it becomes the school leader's responsibility to ensure availability of appropriate, intensive, and effective English language development materials and academic content materials to promote access to the core content. Reform-minded leaders invest in the development and adoption of English language development materials aligned to the ELD standards and designed to address the full continuum of development to English proficiency, including the academic language needs of English learners. Leaders are encouraged to establish criteria for new materials and adopt grade-level academic content texts that have language objectives by English proficiency level tied to the linguistic demands of the texts, and that support differentiated instruction for English learners at various proficiency levels.

Test Your Knowledge

Whether at the elementary or secondary level, all English learner programs presumably include an ELD component. This cornerstone feature is paramount to the academic success of the English learner. Reflect on the following questions regarding the ELD components in your school:

1. What evidence can your school show that demonstrates that English learners are developing English language proficiency?
2. How does your school's ELD program contribute to mastery in content areas for English learners?
3. Is the focus of your ELD program on language objectives or content objectives? Or both?

THE EQUITY ISSUE: ACCESS TO CORE CURRICULUM

Chapter 3 broadly addressed the importance of providing access to core curriculum if the English learner gap is to narrow. The dilemma of how to provide effective ELD instruction to English learners while simultaneously providing access to core curriculum continues to be a challenge for the reform-minded leader. Table 5.1 illustrated the challenge of reconciling the ELD component with the provision of access to core curriculum for English learners at the high school level.

Olsen (2010a) asserts that while acquiring English, English learners have only as much access to the curriculum as the teacher finds ways to make it comprehensible. By definition, an English learner does not have sufficient mastery of English to understand and participate fully in an English-taught curriculum. This means that during the years they are learning English, English learners are only partially learning much of the science, social studies, and language arts that is being taught.

Jencks and Phillips (1998) counsel that in theory, the remediation of curriculum and instruction will bring low-performing students up to par with their peers. In reality, however, low-track placement frequently results in exposure to less rigorous content and fewer learning opportunities than high-track placement. In short, low-track students fall further behind. Perhaps the most visible effect of stratified curriculum and instruction is the much-discussed achievement gap. The contention that course placement is not completely meritocratic (Oakes, 1985) but, rather, the result of social and individual factors gives rise to numerous arguments against stratified instruction. Hence, the equity argument evolves. At its most fundamental level, the equity debate is the quest for providing equal access to core curriculum and instruction to all students.

The equity issue becomes more pronounced as the English learner progresses through the educational system. Earlier chapters showed that schools characterized by poverty, limited resources, and unqualified teachers tend to be populated by large enrollments of English learners. Olsen (2010b) emphasizes that there have long been discrepancies in access and exposure to an enriched curriculum between schools in lower socioeconomic communities and those in wealthier communities, between high-minority enrollment schools and schools with fewer minority groups. The well-documented differences in the presence of school libraries, science labs, technology, experienced teachers, and adequate facilities, the researcher argues, have been a persistent feature of the landscape of unequal education in our nation. Aside from the very crucial issues of equity in this unequal distribution, the development of academic language for English learners is impeded when language development is taught in the absence of a full and enriched curriculum. Language development, the researcher contends, occurs not only through an explicit language arts curriculum but through the use of language as a vehicle for learning academic content and learning about the world. Social studies and science are particularly rich content areas for the development of language.

This obstruction or deference of the core curriculum for English learners comes with consequences. According to Lindholm-Leary and Genesee (2010), in the past decade, several forces have contributed to a narrowed curriculum. For people familiar with second language development research, it seems like common sense that if students are not doing well in English, the time spent teaching them English should be increased. However, more time does not translate to better outcomes.

The result of those beliefs, Olsen (2010b) claims, has been to crowd out other areas of the curriculum to make time for more and more instruction in language arts. Furthermore, in efforts to focus underperforming schools on the essential tasks of teaching English reading and math, a series of misguided state policies and practices have emerged that have also unintentionally resulted in a narrowing of curriculum for students who attend underperforming schools. These are policies of increasing mandated minutes and hours to be spent in language arts and math—crowding out time for other subjects. That the narrowing of the curriculum is having an adverse impact on English learners is not news to the educational community. That this same phenomenon is a cause to the continued widening of the achievement gap is a revelation to many leaders.

This narrowing effect is blatant in some states. In California, a statewide survey in 2009 found that among schools at which the low achievement of the English learner subgroup resulted in the school being placed into Program Improvement status, 65% reported that corrective actions required them to expand the hours of the day spent on English language arts and math, resulting in reduced access to science and social studies. In 17% of the schools, students no longer receive science and social studies at all. In 28% of the schools, English learners do not get art or music at all, and almost half of the schools had reduced art and music as part of their corrective action (Californians Together, 2008).

It is useful to look at the English learner equity issue as the means to an end. The tracking of English learners into substandard English language development paths is the means. The narrowing of the curriculum and its subsequent achievement gap is the end. Perhaps due to moral laziness or ethical coziness, educators will vehemently deny the existence of tracking in their schools. This dynamic is commonly masked behind a variety of labels. Tyack (1974) identified tracking as the assignment of students to differentiated coursework with varying levels of academic content. The theory behind tracking posits that low-performing students must be separated from other students and taught a simplified curriculum.

Olsen (2010b) asserts that states and school districts have a legal and moral responsibility to ensure equal educational access through programs that speak to the needs of all English learners by developing their proficiency to the level required for participation in an English-taught curriculum, and providing access to the core curriculum. The English learner equity issue is addressed again in Chapter 9 as part of a comprehensive model for instructional improvement.

Leadership Compass

Vigil (1997) connects the overall low academic performance of English learners to less than optimal learning environments, low-level academic content, and poor teacher–student relationships. These contexts are exacerbated for English learners in ELD learning environments. Katz's (1999) analysis of the tracking processes common in middle schools shows how English learners are placed in low-track classes with little expected of them, assigned to a physically isolated site, and taught by underprepared teachers in classrooms with limited materials. In such a setting, academic needs cannot help but be left untended. These school environments are portrayed as physically, academically, and socially isolated school contexts for immigrant, minority, and linguistic minority students. This slice of research makes transparent the reality of inequitable opportunity for English learners.

Analyses of the relationships among language proficiency, placement, and achievement have attempted to isolate the effect of English learner status on academic outcomes. Wang and Goldschmidt (1999) found that while students placed in minimum-standards courses scored below all other students, the effect of low-track placement was strongest among English learners. The researchers also found that the marginal effect of being classified as an English learner changes depending upon whether the student was enrolled in a minimum standards mathematics course or high-level coursework. The effect of English learner status on academic performance was minimized among those students placed in higher-track classes, suggesting heightened sensitivity to the quality of academic exposure for these students. These findings imply that, given access to higher-quality curricula, English learners will rise to meet the challenge (Callahan, 2005).

The reform-minded school leader is haunted by the fact that, regardless of the label used, the tracking of English learners is prevalent in schools and is the primary catalyst of the achievement gap. How, then, does the leader ensure that English learners have access to the full curriculum? For starters, the leader is encouraged to collect information and conduct an assessment of the extent of English learner access to the full curriculum in their schools. Is the narrowing of the curriculum a common dynamic in the school? Additionally, the leader should examine the essential program components requirement of instructional minutes for basic core English language arts and math programs to support access to a full curriculum content. There need to be differentiated options that enable a more efficient use of time for English learner students facing the double challenge of mastering a new language and all other academic content (Olsen, 2010b).

Hallinan and Kubitschek (1999) argue that tracking persists even today as a result of the belief that sorting students by ability and assigning curricula accordingly enhances learning; however, a wide range of studies dispute this claim. Academic content is tied directly to the instructional goals of the teacher, and expectations correlate highly with class content. The curricular structure in place in U.S. schools grants access to challenging academic opportunities to some while denying it to others. Both track placement and mobility vary along racial lines suggesting that placement is not wholly meritocratic (Callahan, 2005).

Test Your Knowledge

The narrowing of the curriculum poses tremendous implications for the academic success of English learners. Schools typically overemphasize the ELD component resulting in some content areas falling by the wayside. This catch-22 scenario leads to tracking. Based on this context, reflect on the following:

1. Is there evidence of the narrowing of the curriculum in your school?
2. To what extent are English learners prone to being tracked in your school?
3. What is the "collective philosophy" of your school on the equity issue as it pertains to English learners?

LOST IN THE MAINSTREAM

The previous section argued for examining the equity issue in school and hence ensuring that English learners have access to core curriculum. Paradoxically, however, the English learners placed in the mainstream or the core curriculum will inevitably get lost in the abyss without the proper support. Because of the self-contained structure in elementary schools, the mainstream of English learners does not seem to have the same devastating effects that it has in the secondary schools. In California, Callahan (2006) found the most common program for long-term English learners in secondary schools is placement into mainstream classes designed for and mixed with English-proficient students. Teachers often do not know they have English learners in their classes. There is nothing about these classes (instruction, pacing, curriculum, grouping) that addresses the language development or access needs of long-term English learners. Similarly, in examining the range of English proficiency levels in mainstream classes, Maxwell-Jolly, Gándara, and Mendez-Benavidez (2007) found that many classrooms have students ranging from non-English-proficient (no English) to honors-level students with high academic and native levels of English—and all levels in between. Differentiated instruction is difficult—and made more so when the range in skills is so broad. In these classes, even though a teacher may not be formally aware that some students are English learners, teachers tend to teach toward the middle.

Case (2002) suggests that English learners may face particular challenges when contending with the language demands of subject-matter instruction. For English learners, the challenge of learning specialized disciplinary language is added to the task of learning English. Although the dominant approach to resolving this dilemma has been to delay content-area instruction based on the assumption that English proficiency is a prerequisite for learning content, Cervetti, Bravo, Duong, Hernandez, and Tilson (2008) reject this approach for two reasons. First, learning of content-area knowledge and vocabulary is too important to delay for years until English learners become fully proficient in English. The potential for this approach to provide an enduring academic setback for English language learners is too perilous. Second, there are good reasons to believe that content-area instruction can provide an excellent context for the development of academic English.

Echevarria, Vogt, and Short (2004) found that science, for example, involves the kind of learning through multiple modalities (talking, reading, writing, doing firsthand investigations) that is often touted as characteristic of high-quality instruction for English learners. In addition, attempts to teach academic language—the language of academic disciplines—separately from content-area instruction seems potentially ineffectual. Cervetti et al. (2008) suggest that students learn to read and write science texts best by learning to do so in authentic contexts for authentic purposes.

Leadership Compass

Chapter 1 discussed the characteristics and academic needs of three cohorts of English learners (see Figure 1.3). These English learner cohorts are defined on the basis of length of residency and schooling prior to immigration. Callahan (2005) emphasizes that the academic and linguistic requirements of each of the three cohorts are unique. Recent immigrants with significant amounts of previous schooling have mastered grade-level academic content and often require instruction only in English literacy skills. Having missed more than 1 year of academic instruction in their home country, recent immigrants with limited schooling require literacy skill development and content-area instruction in order to access the high school curriculum.

The most challenging cohort facing school leaders today is the long-term English learner. Long-term English learners, according to Callahan (2005), comprise the largest cohort in California, who make up approximately two-thirds of the English learner population. The remainder of the secondary English learner population is made up of recent immigrants with either low or high levels of previous schooling. It is this cohort of long-term English learners that is drowning in the mainstream and, when closely examined, is overrepresented in the achievement gap. Monitoring the academic progress of long-term English learners is time well spent for the school leader.

Faltis and Wolfe (1999) note that when they are schooled primarily in the United States, long-term English learners are generally orally proficient but have poor reading and writing skills and little control of academic English. Many long-term English learners are unable to exit English learner programs because their academic achievement is not at grade level. Regardless of the academic and linguistic needs of each cohort, tracking English learners limits access to academic and linguistic models and input (Callahan, 2005).

A long-term English learner's schedule tends to be filled with English/English language development (ELD), intervention, support classes, and math. The ELD classes in many districts do not receive university approved credit, so long-term English learners who remain in ELD because their language proficiency scores do not progress beyond intermediate levels cannot earn the English credits for college preparation. The number of intervention and support classes in English and math crowd out access to electives and, in some schools, science and social studies.

The school leader's posture in addressing the needs of English learners in the mainstream classroom is to focus on content-area academic progress and the ELD component simultaneously.

Test Your Knowledge

One side of the English learner argument subscribes to the belief that ELD can and should be the responsibility of the mainstream classroom. However, most mainstream teachers do not see it as their responsibility to handle ELD in their classrooms. Reflect on the following questions pertaining to ELD in your school:

1. What features of ELD can be found in your mainstream classrooms?
2. What are the ranges of your ELs' language proficiency levels in mainstream classrooms?
3. Are your mainstream teachers aware of the English learners in their classrooms? If so, is there an evidence of differentiation of instruction?

SUSTAINABILITY INDICATOR: TEACHER COMMITMENT

Flexible programming is important if English learners are to experience any level of academic success in schools. This chapter has advocated for the leader's role in ensuring that an effective English language development component should be closely monitored and assessed in addition to the assurance of access to core curriculum for English learners. While tending to these school reform dynamics, perhaps the strongest variable at play is the role of teacher commitment in the success of English learners.

Teacher commitment is critical to the success of English learner reform. In examining teacher commitment to reform, Little and Barlett (2002) reveal interesting paradoxes: Reform both stimulates teacher enthusiasm and results in burnout, expands some learning opportunities and erodes others, intensifies professional bonds and foments professional conflict. The role of teacher commitment in education reforms has been well documented in the literature. Day and Gu (2007) assert that teacher commitment involves the interplay of personal, workplace, and education systemic factors, but they also illuminate how these factors interplay differently in teachers with sustained/increased and decreased commitment.

Datnow (2000) writes that teacher commitment at the inception of a reform plays a critical role in the successful implementation of the reform. On the one hand, teachers who are happy with how the reform is working at their school, or whose ideologies match the reform, may be more likely to participate in the reform adoption process. On the other hand, teachers who are not in favor of the reform may be more likely to criticize the adoption process, minimizing their role in it. There are tensions that often exist between teachers who were for and against the reform that may have also contributed to teachers' sense-making about reform adoption.

In providing insights on teacher commitment, and as discussed in an earlier chapter, Choi and Tang (2009) portray the image of a committed teacher as one who gives extra time, thought, and effort for students, school, and teaching; is willing to seek improvement, to do things to an excellent standard; is engaged wholeheartedly, more than merely to fulfill responsibility; and has a vision and strives to do something right for the students. In the case of English learner reform, this teacher commitment manifests in ensuring that English learners are succeeding in the mainstream classroom as well as getting access to core curriculum.

Interestingly, various factors have been found to enhance or diminish teacher commitment. Leithwood, Jantzi, and Steinbach (1999) found that leadership, teacher autonomy, collaboration, feedback, learning opportunities, resources, and participation in decision-making were some crucial factors in sustaining high levels of teacher commitment. Additionally, Ware and Kitsantas (2007) found that principals could minimize teacher stress that arises from excessive state initiatives and community expectations, as an additional effective predictor of teacher commitment.

Getting teachers to commit to addressing the needs of English learners in schools is of particular importance at the implementation phase of a school reform. Some prior research on implementation might suggest that the adoption process is not so important and that once teachers have an opportunity to try a new reform and find it effective, they will support it. How a reform is introduced has a profound impact on the reform's successful implementation (Datnow, 2000).

In providing insights on teacher commitment, the reform-minded leader empowers staff to introspectively examine the flexible program options advocated in this chapter. The various paths outlined here can help a school avoid putting the English learner through the Ping Pong Effect or even a revolving door policy. Whether it is through the assurance of equity, access to core curriculum, or success in the mainstream classroom, the school leader should give careful consideration to ensure that the English learners' academic and language deficits are not the result of a rigid, structural problem in the school.

The rubric shown in Table 5.2 is provided as a tool for school leaders to dialogue with staff on their school's progress in English learner programming.

Table 5.2. Flexible Program Options for English Learner Reform Continuum

Element of English Learner Programming	Emerging Stage	Developing Stage	Sustainability Stage
The ELD Component of Your English Learner Program	The ELD component is in name only and there is little or no effort to provide effective ELD services to English learners. There is no ELD curriculum in place and ELs are making little or no progress in developing English language proficiency.	There is an established ELD component in the school. The ELD pullout model or ELD is the only component in the school day designed to address the needs of English learners. The ELD curriculum is inadequate for meeting the academic needs of ELs.	Teachers work collaboratively in departments or grade levels to build shared knowledge regarding ELD. Mainstream teachers use content to develop English language proficiency in ELs. The ELD component is continuously monitored and evaluated for effectiveness. There is clear evidence that ELs are developing English language proficiency.
English Learner Equity: Access to Core Curriculum	The English learner does not participate fully in an English-taught curriculum. Two or more subjects are deferred as the time in ELD is being increased. English language development is taught in isolation and in absence of a full and enriched curriculum.	One content area is deferred. The English learner is provided a doubled-ELD time but the curriculum is narrowed through the exclusion of science or social studies. There is minimal evidence of collaboration/connections between ELD and content areas.	No content area is deferred, with ELD embedded in the content areas. Mainstream teachers are fully versed and trained in ELD pedagogy and use language as a vehicle for teaching academic content and learning about the world. EL academic achievement data substantiate that ELs are succeeding in the mainstream classroom.
Support in the Mainstream Classrooms	There is a "sink-or-swim" mentality defining EL programming. There are three or more proficiency levels in mainstream classrooms. Teachers are not aware of who the ELs are and there is no effort to address language development in the classroom. The teachers' focus is on content delivery.	Although teachers are cognizant of English learners in their classroom, there are minimal language development opportunities. Instruction is differentiated for the EL but the teacher tends to teach toward the middle. Minimal effort is placed in the EL attainment of academic vocabulary.	Instruction, pacing, curriculum, and classroom grouping are adjusted in mainstream classrooms to address the language development of ELs. Teachers are fully aware of who their ELs are and pay particular attention to the attainment of academic vocabulary and English language development in their classrooms.

Chapter 5 Application Exercises: Examining the Flexibility of Your School's English Learner Programming

Individual Exercise Closely examine Figure 5.1, The Incoherent Schooling of English Learners. Contingent on your school level (elementary, middle, or high school), reflect on the process or path that English learners follow in your school from one grade level to the other. What evidence do you have that indicates that programming for English learners is flexible, allowing for multiple opportunities for English learner success? Can you cite an example in which an English learner fell prey to the Ping Pong Effect?

Team Exercise At your next school leadership team meeting, draw a 3-column chart on the whiteboard. Label the left column "1-Programs"; the middle column "2-Gifted or Honors Students"; and the right column "3-English learners." In column 1, list a least five exemplary academic programs offered at your school. In column 2, place a check by each program that is available to your gifted/honors students. Repeat the process in column 3 by placing a check by each program that is available to your English learners. Is there evidence of any discrepancies in providing equal access to English learners? What would your school look like if both columns 2 and 3 were the same? Is there equity in your school?

School Exercise In schools that tout success with English learners, there is no ambiguity regarding commitment to ELs. Ownership and commitment to ELs are key factors in whether mainstream teachers will address the needs of ELs in content/subject areas. At your next schoolwide staff meeting, have teachers sit at tables of six or fewer, reflecting diverse content areas or grade levels. Have each table discuss the ways in which teacher commitment to ELs is evident in your school and illustrate the best example on chart paper without the use of words. After 10 minutes, have each table group present their work. Summarize the session by highlighting the variety of ways that teacher commitment to English learners is evident in your school. How would these commitments lead to improved English learner academic achievement?

6

Research-Based Instructional Strategies

Enough Is Known to Make a Difference

If we know so well what good instructional strategies are that could counter historic "educational debts," why is it that we have not assured that such strategies are broadly implemented? (Ladson-Billings, 2006, p. 4)

The teaching force in this country's public education system is not adequately trained to meet the academic needs of English learners. The mounting evidence that teachers are not prepared for the changing demographics of their classrooms is validated by Lewis et al. (1999), who found a majority of teachers from urban fringe/large towns (67%), central cities (58%), and rural locales (82%) reporting that they had never participated in professional development for addressing the needs of English learners. Additionally, these researchers discovered that of the 41% of teachers who taught English learners, less than 13% had received 8 or more hours of training in the last 3 years in how to teach English learners.

In addition to lacking adequate training, these teachers also lacked sheltered English learner curricula and materials that could supplement the regular textbook. Furthermore, few research-based interventions for native-English-speaking students have been evaluated as to their efficacy for English learners. Regardless of the program design for English learners, the instruction in the classroom should reconcile the students' second language development needs with their content-knowledge requirements (Short & Fitzsimmons, 2007).

Herein lies the dilemma. Many teachers are not well prepared to integrate language instruction in their content lessons. The lack of teacher training, the lack of resource materials for addressing English learner needs, and the inability of the teacher to develop English language proficiency while delivering content sets the stage for the formation of the public schools' "perfect storm." The public school system in this country is ill-prepared to meet the academic needs of a rapidly increasing English learner population. The pervasive achievement gap is not likely to narrow until these three factors are addressed.

This institutional ineptitude has its origins in educators' myopic view of English learners' limitations in English, overlooking an underutilized instructional tool and a highly desirable skill: English learners' first language literacy. For the most part, English learners are not only limited English speakers; they are, with rare exception, emerging bilinguals (Garcia, Kleifgen, & Falchi, 2008). Unfortunately, unlike our European counterparts, bilingualism in this country's public schools is perceived as a liability rather than an asset—much to the detriment of society.

Hamann and Reeves (2008) assert that in content-area teaching and learning, English learners' access to content learning is diminished when teachers cannot provide instruction in the English learners' native language. Further, the researchers contend, when English learners' bilingual skills are not validated by schools (and, in some cases, are even discouraged), language attrition may ensue and schools' non-acceptance of learners' linguistic identities could imperil their connection to school.

Although instructional strategies that aim for simultaneous English language development and content-area learning for English learners show promise as well as practicality, the English-only approach to English learner instruction that is commonly found in more classrooms than not limits English learners' access to instruction and to fair assessment. There is no evidence that teaching content through a learners' second language (i.e., English) is the most effective approach. In fact, the opposite holds true: Instructing learners in content areas through their strongest language gives learners better access to content-area learning and, importantly, better access to fair, valid, and reliable assessment of what they know and can do in the content areas (Hamann & Reeves, 2008).

Hamann and Reeves (2008) point out that effective, research-based instructional strategies that account for the English learners' primary language have a significant impact on English learners in classrooms in this country. These strategies yield positive educational outcomes, and they are centrally relevant to both existing achievement gaps and the narrowing of those gaps. Olsen (2010b) asserts that the effective application of these instructional strategies inside those classrooms is crucial. The placement of English learners into high-level content courses is contingent on instruction that is designed and adapted to their needs. This classroom dynamic requires that teachers not only know their English learners but also engage in careful analysis of the language demands of the content they are teaching, as well as possess skills in implementing appropriate instructional strategies.

This immense responsibility cannot reside solely with the classroom teacher. A support structure from the school and district level is essential to achieve the aforementioned scenario in the classroom. Olsen (2010a) explores the district's posture in ensuring a solid instructional program for English learners. The researcher argues that the district has a significant role to play to ensure high-quality implementation of research-based programs for English learners through the following: clear descriptions of program models in English learner master plans; ongoing and targeted professional development for teachers and administrators in understanding the needs of English learners and strategies to meet those needs; clarity of expectations about what quality instruction looks like; curriculum materials that facilitate differentiation for varying levels of needs; benchmarks of growth and achievement for English learners; mechanisms for monitoring student progress; and systems for holding staff accountable for high-quality programs for English learners.

In making the case for effective instructional strategies for English learners in the classroom, this chapter champions school leaders' careful attention to and consideration of the dynamics of the instructional process for English learners in the content-area classroom. The premise of this chapter is to lay out a research-grounded depiction of effective instructional strategies for English learners. This chapter describes the importance of:

- Building background knowledge for English learners;
- Effective academic vocabulary instruction; and
- Language development in content-area teaching.

As a way of ensuring that teachers have the required skill set to address these essential components, the element of sustained professional development is highlighted in this chapter as a critical piece of the sustainability framework.

BUILDING BACKGROUND KNOWLEDGE

Marzano's (2004) extensive research on the topic of building background knowledge in students reveals that all learners acquire background knowledge through the interaction of two factors: (1) the processing and storing of information, and (2) the number and frequency of academically oriented encounters. Substantiating this stance, Richard-Amato and Snow (2005) argue that helping English learners retrieve relevant background knowledge facilitates their understanding of the lesson content and increases the likelihood of learning and retention.

Bernhardt (2005) asserts that background knowledge—what students know from schooling, personal experience, or insights gained from study in another country or from oral history—is important because background schema are a major factor in reading comprehension. Short and Fitzsimmons (2007) emphasize that connecting instruction to what the learners know and then explicitly discussing how that knowledge applies to the topic at hand is a technique teachers should use with English learners. For example, the researchers explain, immigrant students may not have studied the U.S. Civil War, but they may have lived through a military conflict at home, and that experience could give them special insight into U.S. history. Other ways to build background involve introducing students to new academic topics through short video clips, demonstrations, or field experiences.

The building of background knowledge becomes increasingly essential as English learners move into secondary schools. Short and Fitzsimmons (2007) make note of the fact that many adolescent English learners lack background knowledge of the topics taught in middle and high school content classes. Teachers must activate what prior knowledge exists and apply it to the lessons or explicitly build background schema. Students who have been in U.S. schools since the early grades generally have some of the background knowledge that is expected by teachers, textbooks, and curricula in the secondary grades, but students who are new to the United States may not.

Hamann and Reeves (2008) contend that activating learners' prior knowledge and utilizing their lived experiences in the instruction of new material can be highly effective, not just because of how it allows for effective scaffolding but also because of the relational affirmation it offers. Valuing and supporting learners' background knowledge helps teachers engage learners during instruction. Too often, the background knowledge of learners from different linguistic and cultural backgrounds has not been received with the same legitimacy as that of English-only learners. Quite often, educators know the historic, cultural, and linguistic experiences of non-White groups less well and thus have fewer starting points for engagement. Moje et al. (2004) maintain that when teachers make an effort to learn about students' existing funds of knowledge, and when they encourage students to relate that knowledge to the subjects studied in class, students tend to become more engaged in the lesson with their reading comprehension improving.

Garcia and Godina (2004) convey that more often than not, both the language and the content taught in schools are new to English learners. Therefore, when language instruction is linked closely to real-life experiences, including the content or themes being taught in other classes, students have more success integrating the two. With teacher facilitation, students can access their content knowledge to bolster their academic language development and similarly use their language skills to gain more content knowledge.

One of the most effective means of building background knowledge in English learners is through the use of cognates. Green (2004) divulges that English learners whose first language is a Romance language, such as Spanish, French, Italian, Portuguese, and Romanian, are not beginning from ground zero when it comes to English language acquisition. These students can often call on their knowledge of cognates in their native language to determine the meaning of the words in their second language. The number of cognates they will encounter tends to increase with the grades as they encounter increasing numbers of words with Latin roots, especially in their science and social studies courses.

From an institutional perspective, it behooves the school leader to articulate the expectation for the use of instructional strategies that make use of cognates in the classroom. Nagy, Garcia, Dyrgunoglu, and Hancin (1993) found that the recognition and use of cognates does not automatically occur for English learners. The teachers in their study were effectively able to teach their students to better use the cognate knowledge that they did possess in their native language—Spanish. Interestingly, the majority of English learners in this country's public schools is made up of Spanish speakers.

Rodríguez (2001) suggests the following steps for teaching Spanish-speaking students to use cognates and context in reading texts in English:

1. Have students read the text silently or aloud to a partner. Discuss what it means with the partner or in a small group.
2. Discuss the vocabulary with the whole class. Use cognates and context clues to figure out meanings. Point out spelling patterns, like "–tion" in English becomes "–ción" in Spanish.
3. Discuss grammatical differences between English and Spanish, such as word order for nouns and adjectives.
4. Read the text aloud as students follow along. Have students listen for words they recognize orally.
5. Read a similar text with Germanic-based words in place of the cognates. Compare.
6. Clarify and explain words in the texts that cannot be figured out from cognates or context.

The importance of building background knowledge in English learners is indisputable, particularly in content-area classes. The use of cognates, as the research has illustrated, is an effective approach for building this background knowledge.

Leadership Compass

Using the English learners' first language for delivering content can play an important role, particularly as background knowledge is being developed. Teachers are not equipped with the skill set to deliver this dual-pronged approach in the instructional process. The teacher's sole use of English for instruction can be a limitation for the English learner. However, an often overlooked resource in schools has been the role of the para-educator in English learner education. In reviewing research literature on English learners, Hamann and Reeves (2008) found a body of work that identified effectiveness in the collaborative instruction of English learners, in which teachers and paraprofessionals (e.g., Spanish-English bilingual teaching aides) work together to deliver effective instruction for English learners. In the case of paraprofessionals who share English learners' first language, not only are the aides able to provide linguistic support, but they also play a pivotal role in the education of language minority students, in spite of the overwhelming demands on their time, fragmented schedules, and minimal pay. School leaders would be wise to recognize and affirm the experiences, insights, knowledge, and abilities of para-educators. Through the effective use of bilingual para-educators, classroom teachers who do not share an English learner's first language have the opportunity to provide content through languages other than English, which can both boost academic achievement as well as validate English learners' cultural and linguistic identities (Ernst-Slavit & Wenger, 2006).

Test Your Knowledge

With the standards-based reform movement came the incessant obsession to cover an enormous amount of content in a short period of classroom instructional time. This drive for coverage has led to classroom lessons that often circumvent the building of background knowledge in English learners. Reflect on the following questions regarding building background knowledge in the English learners in your school:

1. How well versed are your teachers on the research and importance of building background knowledge in English learners?
2. How would you begin to assess your teachers' professional development needs in this arena?
3. As you conduct classroom walkthroughs, how often do you see teachers making an overt effort at utilizing English learners' background knowledge to frame or inform their lesson objective?

ACADEMIC VOCABULARY INSTRUCTION

Content-area courses such as science, social studies, literature, and math are heavily populated with relevant academic vocabulary. One of the biggest cognitive challenges for English learners is the understanding of critical concepts in these content classes. An English learner cannot comprehend a lesson without knowing critical vocabulary (Gersten, Taylor, & Graves, 1999).

Graves (2006) asserts that in order to succeed in school, students need a strong and constantly growing vocabulary base. Knowledge of words, word parts, and word relationships is critical if students are to understand topics in a content area and develop strong reading comprehension and test-taking skills. Many of the English learners in schools come from low-income families and research has unveiled that students from low-income backgrounds tend to have limited academic vocabularies. Hart and Risley (2003) estimated a 30-million-word gap by age 3 between the average number of words heard by the children of parents on welfare and those whose parents are professionals. Additionally, Wolf et al.'s (2008) research has suggested that measuring academic vocabulary is necessary to better predict English learners' readiness for and success in mainstream classrooms.

Wide area reading can mean a dramatic difference in the number of words students are exposed to every year. Anderson, Wilson, and Fielding (1988) found that 30% of children read less than 90 seconds per day outside of school. This means they read 100,000 or fewer words per year. Compare that exposure to the top 2% of readers who read 65 minutes or more per day, reading at least 4,358,000 words a year (Green, 2004). D'Anna, Zechmeister, and Hall (1991) calculated that the average number of words that a high school senior knows ranges from a high of 50,000 to a low of 17,000. This translates to learning 3,000 to 4,000 new words a year for English speakers. Clearly, English learners have an even greater vocabulary acquisition task in front of them (Green, 2004).

English learners, according to Echevarria, Vogt, and Short (2004), can develop academic vocabulary through a variety of methods. Visuals, graphic organizers, demonstrations, and other instructional aids and devices can help students better understand and remember words and their meanings. Also helpful are word attack techniques, such as identifying words in English that are similar and related to those in the student's native language (recall the discussion on cognates in the previous section) and developing clues to the meaning of a word based on context clues and structural analysis. Graves (2006) advocates that teachers teach multiple meanings of words and help students incorporate words into their expressive vocabularies. For English learners, teachers also need to distinguish between content-specific words (e.g., *hypotenuse*, *equilateral*), process words (e.g., *scan*, *draft*, *clarify*), and words related to English structure.

Understanding an academic vocabulary schema helps leaders embed structures in their schools to help English learners develop essential academic vocabulary to experience academic success. As illustrated in Figure 6.1, McKeown and Beck (2005) assert that a mature, literate individual's vocabulary comprises three tiers. Tier One has the most basic words, such as *bed*, *brother*, *sky*, and *run*. Most learners already know the meanings of Tier One words. Tier Two consists of words such as *compromise*, *scrutinize*, *diligent*, and *typical*, which are of high frequency for mature users and are found across a variety of domains. Tier Three consists of rare words such as *apogee*, *precinct*, *peninsula*, and *ecclesiastical*, which tend to be limited to specific domains. The researchers found that instruction directed at Tier Two words is the most productive. A sound vocabulary development program that takes into account this three-tiered schema helps teachers determine which words to teach and to what depth. This approach should also incorporate a number of innovative vocabulary development techniques that the researchers call rich instruction to produce deep word knowledge required for comprehension. Gersten et al. (1999) explain that an effective approach to vocabulary development uses short, explicit class segments when the teacher directly teaches key vocabulary.

Figure 6.1. Academic Vocabulary Schema

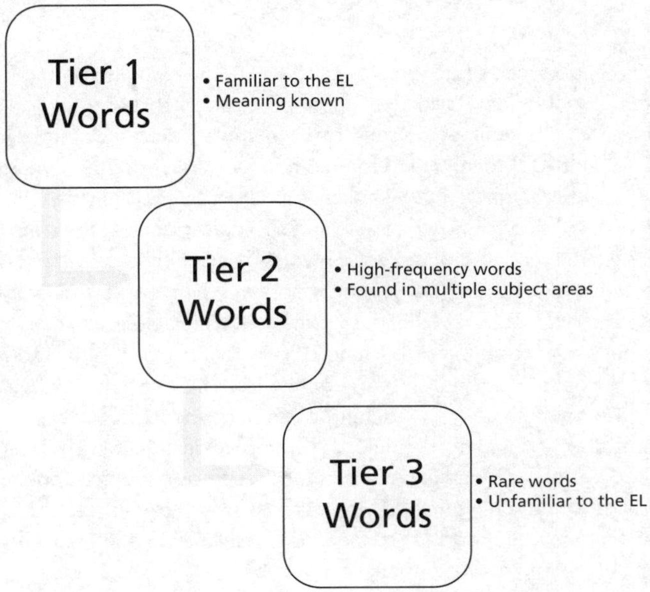

The three-tiered structure to vocabulary development is supported by the work of Lesaux, Kieffer, Faller, and Kelley (2010). The researchers identified three guiding principles of vocabulary instruction: (1) vocabulary instruction should be characterized by the promotion of deep understanding of a relatively small number of words, their elements, and semantically and morphologically related words in rich contexts; (2) the words to be taught deeply should be very high-utility in nature; specifically, the words taught should be general-purpose academic words (e.g., *analyze*, *frequent*, *abstract*); and (3) effective vocabulary instruction requires balance between direct teaching and teaching word-learning strategies to equip students with cognitive tools to learn words independently.

Because of the large number of words individuals need to learn, and more so for English learners, direct instruction cannot be used to teach the meaning of all words that students will encounter during their school years. Students must be taught how to acquire word meanings independently, both as they hear new words and as they encounter them in reading. They need to be encouraged to read as widely as possible to be exposed to a greater quantity and variety of words (Green, 2004). The reader is reminded of the effective use of cognates to help English learners further develop their vocabulary foundation.

Leadership Compass

Realizing the importance of academic vocabulary development for English learners, the school leader's attention is now directed at ensuring that an academic vocabulary program becomes a strong focus in content-area teaching. Graves and Watts-Taffe (2002) recommend four components to a vocabulary instruction program: (1) wide reading so that implicit learning can occur; (2) teaching individual words; (3) teaching word-learning strategies; and (4) fostering word consciousness. The teaching of individual words is most effective when learners are given both definitional and contextual information, when learners actively process the new word meanings, and when they experience multiple encounters with words.

To further knowledge in establishing a solid foundational structure for academic vocabulary for English learners, the National Reading Panel (2000) described five main methods of teaching academic vocabulary: (1) explicit instruction, such as providing definitions; (2) implicit instruction (exposure as students read widely); (3) multimedia methods, such as graphic representations and hypertext; (4) capacity methods in which practice is emphasized to make reading automatic; and (5) association methods in which learners draw connections between known and unknown words.

In the same vein, Green (2004) found that vocabulary knowledge is significantly increased by multiple exposures to words in a variety of rich contexts, making connections with other reading material or oral language, pre-instruction of word meanings before reading, and active engagement of the learner in acquiring and using vocabulary.

Lastly, Lesaux et al. (2010) advocate for several features of the program lessons and activities to promote student knowledge, including frequent encounters with the words across contexts; the use of definitional and contextual information to learn and determine word meanings; a balance of direct instruction in word meanings with teaching cognitive strategies for word learning; and the crucial element of designing lessons to promote the active processing of target word meanings.

To ensure that the attainment of academic vocabulary for English learners is not left up to chance, the school leader both builds the structure for the program as well as it monitors it to ensure that research-based strategies are being addressed in the classroom.

Test Your Knowledge

Development of academic vocabulary in the content areas poses one of the biggest challenges for English learners. Schools with high English learner populations should ensure that a solid academic vocabulary program is embedded in all grade levels. Reflect on the following questions:

1. How do your teachers approach the teaching of academic vocabulary to English learners? Is this approach traditionally characterized by asking the English learner to look up the definition of a word?
2. What role does the attainment of academic vocabulary play in your English learners' performance on standardized tests?
3. How would you go about institutionalizing a systematic academic vocabulary instructional program in your school?

LANGUAGE DEVELOPMENT IN CONTENT-AREA TEACHING

Hamann and Reeves (2008) argue that what is needed for English learners to be successful at school is instruction that methodically incorporates English language development as well as subject-matter knowledge. For English learners, however, that language acquisition task is much more acute. English learners have a so-called double burden in U.S. schools. They must learn the knowledge of their content areas and they must simultaneously develop their English language skills (Short & Fitzsimmons, 2007). As a result, it is, perhaps, unsurprising that English learners are not performing as well as their English-proficient peers. Effective instructional strategies must attend to English learners' linguistic and academic needs, and the most promising strategies are those that embed English language development into content learning (Hamann & Reeves, 2008).

Richard-Amato and Snow (2005) define language development as the curricular modifications that a teacher consistently and strategically employs to evoke listening, speaking, reading, and writing at the students' current English language level. In order for English language development to be effective, students' level of language development must be assessed and appropriate questions and activities developed to promote continued progress. Taking on a slightly different perspective, Graves (1987) contends that sound English language development will yield the academic skills necessary for success in school. In order to increase the success rate of English learners, the teacher can divide the objectives for each lesson into three categories: language skills, content skills, and thinking/study skills.

Peregoy and Boyle (2008) emphasize that in creating opportunities for active processing, an effective English language development lesson integrates the four basic language skills—listening, speaking, reading, and writing—to enrich English learners' opportunities to learn. In addition to addressing the four dimensions of language development, the teacher incorporates the use of collaborative learning activities, given the strong sociolinguistic evidence for the benefits of peer interaction for language and metacognitive development (Lesaux et al., 2010). Figure 6.2 illustrates the structure that teachers of English learners navigate in each of the four domains of language development so that optimal language development and content-knowledge opportunities are presented to the English learner.

Optimal learning conditions occur when English learners recognize the relevance of what they are learning. Moje et al. (2004) assert that helping English learners understand how the acquisition of language and academic literacy skills will allow them to achieve at higher levels in other classes may make them more motivated. In a learning environment that incorporates language development with content or themes, students can see for themselves the importance of literacy skills in understanding the way material is presented and how texts are organized. The literacy skills needed to do science, for example, can be made clear and explicitly taught while students are engaged in doing science for a real purpose. Additionally, providing content or theme-based instruction gives English learners an important framework for assimilating new information and applying language skills learned across the curriculum (Echevarria, Short, & Powers, 2006).

Figure 6.2. Language Development and Content Attainment Optimizer

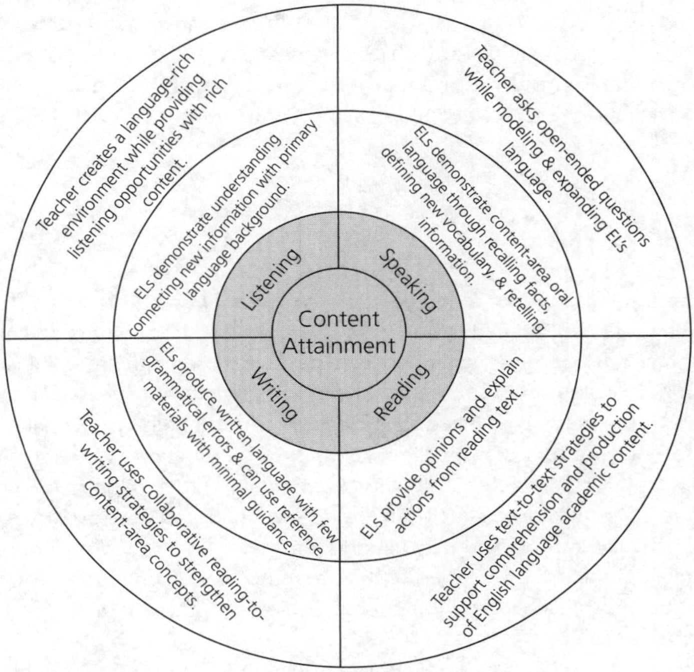

For example, Cervetti, Bravo, Duong, Hernandez, and Tilson (2008) assert that carefully crafted science instruction can not only obviate many of the obstacles that English learners face in learning science, but it can also have particular benefits for their development of academic English language and their ability to navigate the reading and writing assignments that shape their school lives. The researchers further contend that English learners can benefit from instructional approaches that amplify the language of science without watering down the content. Tools such as visual representations (e.g., concept maps, t-charts), inclusion of supplementary materials (books, maps, illustrations), and pre-teaching science vocabulary are commonly suggested language accommodations that scaffold English learners' science experiences.

Although reconciling English language development accommodations in content learning in the classroom makes sense in theory, this dynamic proves to be challenging for the teacher in practice. In their research on English learner accommodations, Cervetti et al. (2008) concluded that (1) the research is often sparse, prompting the formulation of conclusions on a thin base of evidence; (2) the research is often conducted with learners at different stages of development and in contexts other than content-area learning, prompting the use of collective professional judgment to decide how to apply this work to the curriculum development process; and (3) many of the approaches and practices that are most often advocated in the practitioner-oriented literature are untested, so, though they may be effective, further research is needed in this arena.

Leadership Compass

For simultaneous language and content instruction of English learners, Hamann and Reeves (2008) highlight the use of sheltered instruction in the content-area classroom. Sheltered instruction teaches grade-level content through linguistically appropriate instructional strategies. Sheltered instruction classrooms may be English learner–only or a mix of English learner and English-proficient learners. The use of a program of instructional strategies for language and content learning, such as the SIOP (Sheltered Instruction Observation Protocol) instructional model, seems to be particularly effective in the instruction of English learners. An array of linguistically appropriate accommodations gives English learners access to curriculum and learning. Strategies that open access to content through multiple pathways and simultaneously build English learners' English language proficiency are most desirable.

The elements of the research-based SIOP model warrant a school leader's consideration. As a sheltered instructional framework, this model is defined by the following attributes: (1) lesson preparation—using content and language objectives; (2) building background—accessing background knowledge and prior learning; (3) comprehensible input—using clear speech and explanations; (4) strategies—scaffolding learning and opportunities for learning strategy use; (5) interaction—varying grouping configurations and opportunities for peer interaction; (6) practice/application—utilizing hands-on learning and application of knowledge; (7) lesson delivery—matching instruction to instructional objectives; and finally, (8) review and assessment—adequate and appropriate review, assessment, and feedback (Hamann and Reeves, 2008).

Test Your Knowledge

The double burden that English learners face in having to learn English while learning the content poses tremendous challenges for the classroom teacher.

However, ignoring one at the expense of the other serves only to further widen the academic achievement gap for ELs. Reflect on the following questions:

1. Where do you gauge your teachers' skill set in embedding English language development into content learning for English learners?
2. Do you see overt efforts by your teachers in developing English language proficiency in English learners while teaching content?
3. What may be some barriers to institutionalizing the SIOP model in your school?

SUSTAINABILITY INDICATOR: SUSTAINED PROFESSIONAL DEVELOPMENT

As part of the pool of research-based instructional strategies, this chapter has highlighted the importance of building background knowledge of English learners, the need for effective academic vocabulary instruction for English learners, and the importance of English language development in content-area teaching. Although undoubtedly a dire requirement for narrowing the English learner achievement gap, this menu is a tall order for the school leader who is interested in English learner reform in his or her school. This remaining section hones in on that caustic dynamic in schools that, though undisputedly needed, is often maligned for its ineffectiveness—professional development.

Loucks-Horsley, Love, Stiles, Mundry, and Hewson (2003) describe professional development as a process of design that engages teachers in the context of their own classrooms, that aims at strengthening content and pedagogical knowledge while providing opportunities for collaboration and experiences that engage teachers as learners.

Kruse's (2008) research suggests that how professional development is addressed ultimately influences the success or failure of school reforms. Although efforts to improve teaching and learning are at the core of reforming low-performing schools, such efforts are often impaired by mitigating factors such as partially implemented reforms, mixed capacity to foster professional learning, and limited distributed leadership that inhibits large-scale change.

The relationship between student learning and professional development experiences has long been debated in the research. Rivet and Krajcik's (2004) research found a positive relationship between effective professional development programs and student outcomes. Over the years, the researchers contend, some professional development efforts that were focused on standards-based instruction resulted in improved achievement for students.

Czerniak, Beltyukova, Struble, Haney, and Lumpe (2005) revealed that state and federal agencies have invested millions of dollars to develop, implement, and conduct research on effective professional development programs for teachers, perhaps as a response to intense accountability scrutiny. The researchers' findings indicate that sustained professional development experiences that include several (if not all) teachers from a building result in improved instructional practices and increased student learning. Johnson (2007), however, asserts that even though effective professional development models exist, there are still problems with access. Many schools are never provided the opportunity by their respective district to participate in an effective professional development program. Additionally, for those who do participate in an effective program, experiences must be sustained and collaborated at the local level. The researcher argues that after funding for a program is exhausted, reform efforts, including opportunities to collaborate with others, end in most cases. This professional development problem must be addressed if English learner reform is to be sustained.

Understanding the fundamental structural work required for effective professional development is only half of the job. The other half of the task requires school leaders to understand the essential components of what constitutes effective teacher professional development. Bell and Gilbert (1996) found that focus must be placed on teachers' personal, professional, and social development in order for the professional development experience to be successful. In their study of teachers engaged in sustained professional development, three phases emerged. In the first phase, in order for professional growth to take place, teachers needed to grapple with their current practice and to realize that it may have room for improvement. In the second phase, teachers must realize the benefit of moving away from isolation and becoming more collaborative practitioners with others, stepping out of their comfort zones and implementing new strategies. The third phase requires teachers to acknowledge the restraints that may be challenged through the change process such as giving students more control of their learning and dealing with administration and others who may not share the same beliefs about instruction. Once teachers internalize this path, they begin to experience the rewards of collaboration and may seek it out more readily. Through the process of gaining competence with new strategies, teachers become more skilled and confident and may begin to feel more empowered to make a difference.

Fishman, Marx, Best, and Tal (2003) further expanded on how professional development programs are conceptualized. They argued for the need to explicitly explore the connections between the professional development program, teacher classroom practice, and the link to student learning. The researchers maintain that it is no longer acceptable to focus solely on teacher change when the ultimate goal of improving practice is increased student learning. The teacher emphasis of their research framework was the knowledge, beliefs, and attitudes gained from participation in the program and how these were reflected in actual classroom practice. Teachers' beliefs about how to teach and how students learn are key in determining whether or not instructional practices change as a result of the professional development program and whether the change will be sustained.

Hamann and Reeves (2008) unveiled a body of research regarding instructional strategies that point to how to improve learning outcomes for students. The policy task is to figure out the professional development strategy that will convince faculty of both the imperative of pursuing new learning and the viability of that learning for improving practice. But it is the learners themselves (in this case, teachers) who will have to concur that new ways are indeed viable. By focusing on the learning of both teachers and students, Kruse (2008) suggests that when learning is a primary focus of reform, it has the potential to permeate the school culture in ways that foster sustainable improvement.

Undergirding the importance and the critical components of sustained professional development, this chapter has focused on the research-based instructional strategies needed for successful English learner reform. This work has laid out a research-grounded depiction of and justification for ensuring that schools interested in effectively addressing English learner academic needs must attend to the following: building background knowledge in English learners, institutionalizing an effective academic vocabulary instructional program, and ensuring that English language development is not left up to chance in content-area teaching. The next chapter highlights the development of a coherent literacy strategy for English learner success.

The rubric shown in Table 6.1 is provided as a tool for school leaders to dialogue with staff on your school's progress in English learner programming.

Table 6.1. Research-Based Instructional Strategies in English Learner Reform

Element of English Learner Programming	Emerging Stage	Developing Stage	Sustainability Stage
Building Background Knowledge in English Learners	The building of background knowledge in ELs is not addressed/discussed in the school. Classroom instruction is focused solely on content delivery by teachers with little or no effort to use ELs' existing funds of knowledge to make connections. Teachers make no use of cognates and minimal or no professional development is provided.	Teachers know of the importance of building background knowledge in ELs but there is minimal evidence in the classroom. Strategies to tap into ELs' prior knowledge are used sporadically by teachers and the delivery of content takes precedence. There is occasional use of cognates to help ELs develop academic language. Some professional development on the topic has been provided to teachers.	The building of background knowledge in ELs is effectively used by teachers to scaffold learning. Content and language instruction are linked to real-life experiences, including content taught in other curriculum areas. Teachers bolster ELs' academic language development and content knowledge by using cognates in their lessons. Ongoing professional development is provided.

A Systematic Academic Vocabulary Instructional Program	There is no schoolwide program for teaching academic vocabulary to ELs. The attainment of academic vocabulary is traditionally characterized by ELs being asked to look up the definition of words. Teachers have not been trained on effective vocabulary instruction that requires a balance between direct teaching and teaching word-learning strategies.	The teaching of academic vocabulary to ELs is seen in some classrooms and not in others. While some training on teaching academic vocabulary has been provided to teachers, evidence of classroom practice is inconsistent. The use of strategies for academic vocabulary is sporadic across the school, with the attainment of academic vocabulary in ELs left up to chance.	There is a solid systematic program or approach to teaching academic vocabulary to ELs. There is consistent classroom evidence of teachers using association methods in teaching academic vocabulary in which ELs demonstrate connections between known and unknown words. Teachers use visuals, graphic organizers, demonstrations, and other instructional aids to help ELs understand academic vocabulary with a healthy balance between direct teaching and word-learning strategies. There is a sustained professional development program for academic vocabulary in the school.
Language Development in Content-Area Teaching	Teachers have not been trained on strategies for developing language while teaching content. There is little or no evidence of language development strategies for ELs in the classroom. The four basic language skills of listening, speaking, reading, and writing are not used to enrich ELs opportunities to learn. Collaborative language activities for ELs are nonexistent.	Accommodations for English language development are evident in some classrooms as a result of some professional development provided to teachers. Teachers occasionally use listening, speaking, reading, and writing to develop English language in ELs. Some of the lessons contain both content and language objectives.	There is consistent evidence across the school that teachers embed language development skills into their content-area instruction. The four basic language development skills (listening, speaking, reading, and writing) are systematically used by teachers to ensure EL interaction in language and content development. English language development accommodations in content learning are implemented schoolwide.

Chapter 6 Application Exercises:
Examining the Research-Based Instructional Strategies Available to English Learners in Your School

Individual Exercise Kruse (2008) suggests that the failure or success of school reform is contingent on the quality of professional development. The researcher argues that when learning (both for teachers and students) is made the focus of reform, it has the potential to sustain school improvement efforts. Reflect on the professional development program in your school. How is your professional development for teachers addressing the academic needs of English learners? What evidence can you provide that shows that your professional development program is aligned with your school improvement efforts? Are there any disconnects? Why?

Team Exercise During your next grade-level or department meeting, host a conversation with your teachers on the importance of having a systematic approach to teaching academic vocabulary to address the needs of English learners in your school. In collaboration with your staff, devise a simple 3- to 4-step process of how you and your team would go about developing a schoolwide plan to teach academic vocabulary. (Note: An excellent resource to consider for this exercise includes the text *Building Academic Vocabulary: Teacher's Manual* by Robert Marzano and Debra Pickering.)

School Exercise During your next schoolwide staff meeting, give your teachers an opportunity to discuss their take on strategies for building background knowledge in English learners. In tables with job-alike groups, using a round-robin format, have your teams address the following questions: What high-leverage approaches can be used to build background knowledge in English learners? How can and should prior knowledge be activated in English learners? What type of higher-order questioning can be utilized to make learning more relevant for English learners? As a culminating activity, have a spokesperson report on the findings for each group.

7

Coherent Literacy Strategy

Gateway to English Learner Academic Success

> *Far too few programs serving large numbers of . . . ELLs graduate these students with adequate levels of literacy achievement in English. Because of the paucity of research demonstrating outcomes for these students, programs wishing to make research-based reforms have little published or definitive work to guide them. (Short & Fitzsimmons, 2007, p. 39)*

In a literacy research review by the National Literacy Panel on Language-Minority Children and Youth, August and Shanahan (2006) found that direct teaching of the key components of reading plays a critical role, but it is not sufficient for teaching language minority students to read and write proficiently in English, implying that additional work in developing English learner literacy is required. The programs and approaches used in literacy intervention programs designed for native English speakers undoubtedly help English learners to some degree, but they are lacking when it comes to addressing English learners' unique literacy needs. The achievement gap will continue to widen if the specific literacy needs of English learners are not adequately addressed.

The intense accountability scrutiny in the nation's public schools, coupled with the prevailing achievement gap between English learners and non–English learners, has served as a catalyst for researchers and educators to take a closer look at how to help English learners attain English proficiency while mastering academic content. NCLB's focus on the academic performance of English learners, as opposed to simply basic language proficiency development, has sparked an interest in the issue of English learner literacy in schools (Edvantia, 2007).

In examining effective approaches to improving the literacy development of young English learners, August and Shanahan (2006) concluded that the scarcity of rigorous experimental studies on instruction of the components of literacy and the lack of replication studies of central constructs make it difficult to generalize findings and therefore effectively reform the English learner literacy arena.

Slavin and Cheung (2003) note that it is in the earliest years of formal education that children are set on a learning trajectory, contingent on their reading success. These early, formative elementary years are critical for English learners, as it is at this time that they are most likely to be struggling both to learn a new language and to learn to read. Perhaps because of this essential stage in literacy development, the largest number of literacy studies is focused on the early elementary grades.

Genesee, Lindholm-Leary, Saunders, and Christian (2006) argue that without question, a lot more is known about English learner literacy at the elementary level than at the middle and high school levels. Two prominent national panels have highlighted research relevant to English learner literacy. Snow, Burns, and Griffin (1998) reviewed the National Reading Panel's work with more than 450 studies and found that only 17 studies addressed instruction for English learners, with even fewer focusing on secondary school students. Concomitantly, the National Literacy Panel, according to the researchers, examined 309 studies of language minority students aged 3 to 18 acquiring literacy in a societal language and concluded that less than 10% of the studies that focused on classroom instruction targeted students in grades 6 to 12. The secondary English learner literacy research vacuum is indisputable.

Adding to the disparity between the elementary and secondary English learner literacy development research is the element of poverty. In discussing English learner literacy the poverty variable cannot be ignored. Capps et al. (2005) point out that about two-thirds of English learners are from low-income families. The link between poverty and student achievement was examined by Rumberger and Tran (2006), who found that students who attended non–Head Start programs had higher literacy scores at kindergarten entry than students who attended Head Start or who did not attend preschool. English learners, according to the researchers, were less likely than non–English learners to attend non–Head Start programs.

The English learner literacy challenge faced by the rapidly growing student population in this country's public school system calls for an immediate and intense focus on literacy development for English learners. In developing a coherent literacy strategy as a reform effort for a school, it is important for the leader to recognize the critical role that literacy development plays for English learner academic success. In the absence of this vital foundation, the academic success of English learners in their schooling career is doubtful. To that end, this chapter examines the following leadership considerations in the advancement of a literacy strategy for English learners:

- The English learner literacy challenge;
- Second language literacy; and
- Literacy building blocks.

The role of teacher retention as a means of sustaining a sound literacy approach is highlighted in this chapter as a factor in the sustainability framework.

THE ENGLISH LEARNER LITERACY CHALLENGE

Hamann and Reeves (2008) assert that language, in oral and written forms, is the gateway skill set for managing the language of schooling. This gateway toolbox is crucial for acquiring content knowledge and developing the habits of mind needed for effective participation in school. Some academic literacy skills are unique to a certain content area while others are cross-cutting, and these include proficiency in all language modalities—written as well as oral.

How to sort out the individual student traits from those commonly shared by English learners is one of the challenges school leaders face in conceptualizing a literacy strategy. The literacy problems facing English learners are similar to the literacy issues that confront native English speakers. The issue, however, is that schools often delay reading interventions for English learners, assuming that their reading skills will develop as their English proficiency increases (Edvantia, 2007).

Interestingly, August (2003) does not advocate English-only instruction in literacy for English learners. The literacy skills acquired by English learners are a first language transfer to their second language. In a thought-provoking revelation, Collier and Thomas (1989 as cited in August, 2003) reported that children who had attended school and learned basic literacy skills in a native language before emigrating to the United States achieved academic parity with peers as soon as they had acquired proficiency in English in U.S. schools. In contrast, younger children showed long-lasting negative effects on academic achievement associated with initial literacy instruction in English. Slavin and Cheung (2003) argue that whether they are taught in their native language or English, English learners have been found to benefit from instruction in comprehensive reform programs using systematic phonics, one-to-one or small-group tutoring programs, cooperative learning programs, and programs emphasizing extensive reading. Regardless of which approach is undertaken, English learners must be given every opportunity to become competent English readers for the sole reason that literacy is so important to all academic areas.

The English learner literacy issue in schools is complex at the least and daunting at the most. Thomas and Collier (1997) estimate that 30–40% of school-age English learners fail to reach acceptable levels of English reading by the end of their elementary schooling. For some adolescent English learners, failure to attain grade-level competence in reading persists well beyond high school.

As earlier chapters demonstrated, middle and high school teachers face a conundrum in meeting the academic needs of English learners. That large numbers of English learners are enrolling in their schools more than ever before is indisputable. That these secondary teachers are responsible for these students' learning and academic literacy development with little or no training makes for an overwhelming task. Meltzer and Hamann (2006) found that 43% of the teachers polled in their study have at least one English learner enrolled in their classes. These teachers must play a role in bringing students' content-area reading, writing, and thinking skills—in English— up to speed, whether they are monolingual, bilingual, or even trilingual speakers.

Elementary Literacy

In the framing of a literacy strategy for English learners, it is important for leaders to develop a foundational knowledge based on the literacy literature. The research on English learner literacy can be categorized into three distinct sections: elementary reading, middle school reading, and high school reading. In the elementary category, Nunnery et al. (as cited in Slavin & Cheung, 2003) found that Success for All, a comprehensive reform model, in its Spanish bilingual form, yielded positive effects on students' Spanish reading performance (in comparison to schools that taught in Spanish using alternative methods). Additionally, Calderón, Hertz-Lazarowitz, and Slavin (1998) in their 2-year evaluation of Bilingual Cooperative Integrated Reading and Composition, a cooperative learning strategy, found strong positive effects on the Spanish and English reading of children transitioning from Spanish to English reading in grades 2–3. Similarly, Saunders and Goldenberg (1999) found positive results in a transition program for English learners moving to English-only instruction (Slavin & Cheung, 2003). These studies reflect the primary focus of literacy research at the elementary level: that reading skills taught in an English learner's primary language will transfer to English.

Middle School Literacy

At the middle school level, much of the literacy research appears to focus on the important role that vocabulary plays in literacy development.

Scarcella (2003) writes that some English learners enroll in U.S. schools at kindergarten and that by middle school, few of them need instruction in basic English, yet many lack the academic English vocabulary essential for literacy development. Limited vocabulary knowledge is a potential source of reading comprehension difficulties, especially among older, struggling readers, whether they are English learners or not (Lesaux et al., 2010).

Lesaux et al. (2010) examined the dynamics of vocabulary instruction by evaluating the effects of a vocabulary program in low-performing middle schools with high numbers of English learners. The goal of the program was to bolster students' vocabulary and reading comprehension skills. The researchers found positive program effects and concluded that the multicomponent curriculum program was a promising approach for mainstream, urban classrooms with high populations of English learners.

Expanding the research in this arena, Kaufman (1968 as cited in Slavin & Cheung, 2003) evaluated a program in which low-achieving Spanish-speaking 7th-graders were randomly assigned to bilingual or English-only conditions in two New York junior high schools. One school participated in the program for a year and the other for 2 years. In the bilingual classes, students received three or four periods of Spanish reading instruction each week, while controls were in art, music, or health education. On standardized tests of word and paragraph meaning, there were no significant differences in the 2-year school, but in the 1-year school significant differences favored the bilingual group on one- or two-word meaning tests. Results of paragraph meaning tests favored the bilingual group. The vital role that vocabulary development plays in middle school literacy is not to be discounted by school leaders investing in a sound literacy strategy in middle schools.

High School Literacy

Biancarosa and Snow (2006) advocate that a step toward effective reform to increase adolescent literacy rates is the development of empirically based approaches to promote students' reading comprehension skills. When considering literacy at the secondary level, Orellana (2004) argues that adolescent English learners often employ literacy knowledge outside of school that is often not readily apparent in school practices or indicated by school assessments. For instance, students use the Internet, send emails and text messages, listen to music, and read magazines. Students also engage in sophisticated literacy skills such as paraphrasing, interpreting, and translating when asked to read English texts for family members. Minimal research has been done to examine the effects of these practices on literacy development (Short & Fitzsimmons, 2007).

In a study researching high school literacy, 200 low-achieving Mexican American 9th-graders were randomly assigned to bilingual or English-only classes. The bilingual classes involved the use of Spanish in reading, English, and math. Although the pre-test for the groups' scores reflected similar results, the bilingual students scored significantly better on the post-test using the Stanford Diagnostic Reading Test (Covey, 1973, as cited in Slavin & Cheung, 2003). The studies focused on the use of native language instruction with low-achieving English learners in secondary schools and how it may positively impact them with English reading (Slavin & Cheung, 2003).

Albeit scarce, recommendations can be gleaned from the high school English learner literacy research. The literacy instruction for English learners that secondary school teachers have typically used do not appear to facilitate learning. For example, lectures and proverbial worksheets do not provide effective learning scaffolds for these English learners. Textbook features intended to aid student understanding may have the opposite result for students who do not know how to use bolded words, headings, sidebars, and graphs. Many English learners with weak literacy skills have difficulty tracking the flow of information on cluttered text pages (Short & Fitzsimmons, 2007).

Table 7.1 reflects the inferences that can be made from the English learner literacy research. Lesaux et al. (2010) argue for further research focusing on effective instructional practices to promote vocabulary development as it relates to comprehending and analyzing texts in the middle and

Table 7.1. Research Synthesis of English Learner Literacy

Elementary Reading	First language literacy skills appear to transfer to English in the early grades (Slavin & Cheung, 2003). Native language instruction in literacy transfers later (Saunders & Goldberg, 1999).
Middle School Reading	Academic English vocabulary is essential for literacy development (LeSaux et al., 2010). Bilingual reading instruction may have a positive effect on vocabulary development (Kaufman, 1968).
High School Reading	Native language instruction with low-achieving English learners may have a positive effect on English reading (Slavin & Cheung, 2003). Literacy instruction for English learners employed by secondary teachers does not appear to enhance learning (Short & Fitzsimmons, 2007).

high school years. Meltzer and Hamann (2006) contend that in addition to research, more time for quality professional development in content-area literacy is warranted particularly for middle-level and high school teachers.

Leadership Compass

The previous chapter examined the professional development element of the sustainability framework as a tool for institutionalizing research-based instructional strategies. This segment expands deeper into this important concept from a literacy perspective. Without a doubt, literacy is the medium for academic success for all students but more so for English learners. Yet, teachers lack the foundational knowledge to address the literacy development of English learners in their classrooms.

Grant and Wong (2003) critique the inadequate preparation of teachers to deal with English learner literacy and argue that the university preparation programs are responsible for some of the barriers to literacy development for English learners. The researchers contend that two barriers to literacy are the failure of (1) teacher education programs to adequately prepare reading specialists to work with language minority learners and (2) education researchers to engage in more substantive research on English reading development for such students.

If higher education is not properly preparing teachers for meeting the literacy demands of English learners, what should professional development look like for the already practicing teachers? Meltzer and Hamann (2006) maintain that quality content-area literacy professional development should include explicit instruction and modeling of before, during, and after reading strategies; relevance and connections to students' lives; and multiple opportunities for reading, writing, and speaking about content in all classes. These practices, according to the researchers, fall into one of three categories: classroom practices that increase student motivation and engagement, generic literacy and learning practices, and content-specific literacy practices able to better meet the needs of English learners who attend mainstream content-area classes.

Solidifying this stance, in their research on effective reading instruction for English learners, Slavin and Cheung (2003) call for the development of well-justified standards of evidence to learn about effective reading instruction for this distinct population of students. The researchers advocate for a focus on language of instruction as well as on replicable programs intended to improve the reading achievement of English learners. The researchers aim to inform practitioners and policymakers about the tools they have at hand to help all English Language learners learn to read.

Test Your Knowledge

The gap between English learners and non–English learners will continue to widen if school leaders do not begin to address the issue of English learner literacy. Consider the following questions in internalizing the English learner literacy challenge:

1. What percent of your English learners are reading at or below grade level? How effective are the English learner literacy interventions that your school is providing?
2. What is the collective attitude of your teachers with regard to English learner literacy? What role do they see themselves playing in developing literacy skills in English learners?
3. How effective is the literacy professional development that is provided to your teachers?

SECOND LANGUAGE LITERACY

A sound, coherent English learner literacy strategy requires an understanding of second language literacy. Understanding the development of second language literacy skills requires consideration of four variables: (1) the complexity of the reading process, (2) English learner individual differences, (3) linguistic and cognitive development, and (4) the context in which second language learners develop reading (August & Shanahan, 2006).

The issue of English learner literacy or second language literacy is complicated. Slavin and Cheung (2003) write that researchers who study reading instruction for English learners have long attempted to address the issue of whether English learners learn to read in the same way as those who are proficient in English. These researchers have concluded that the factors that lead to reading in English learners are similar to those for their English-proficient classmates. One such factor, according to August (2002, as cited in Slavin & Cheung, 2003), is the role that oral language proficiency plays in literacy development. Oral English proficiency has been found to be highly correlated with English reading.

Substantiating these findings, the National Reading Panel (2000, as cited in Slavin & Cheung, 2003) identified five major elements that contribute to early reading success among English-proficient children: phonemic awareness, phonics, vocabulary, comprehension, and fluency. Not surprisingly, these same factors have also been linked to English reading success for English learners. While accommodations in developing literacy are necessary for English learners, effective reading instruction for English language learners may be similar to effective instruction for English-proficient children, whether the English learners are first taught in their native language or in English (Slavin & Cheung, 2003).

For reform-conscious leaders, the question of the appropriate language of instruction in effective reading programs for English learners is to be kept at the forefront. One school of thought is exemplified by Reese, Garnier, Gallimore, and Goldenberg (2000), who argue that English learners should be taught to read in their native language first while they are learning to speak English, avoiding inevitable failure if children are asked to learn both oral English and English reading at the same time. These English learners are then transitioned to English-only instruction when their English is sufficient to ensure success, usually in 3rd or 4th grade. Native language instruction advocates argue that without native language instruction, English learners are likely to lose their native language proficiency, a critical foundation for literacy development. A contrasting school of thought argues that native language instruction interferes with or delays English language development, and relegates children who receive such instruction to a second-class, separate status within the school. Opponents of native language instruction, it should be noted, are concerned not so much about the use of native language, but about the delay of the use of English along with all its implications (Slavin & Cheung, 2003). Perched between these two camps are English learners, whose literacy development needs go unaddressed.

Slavin and Cheung (2003) contend that teaching reading in two languages, with appropriate adaptations of the English program for the needs of English learners, serves to reconcile the ongoing debates about bilingual education. Proponents of bilingual education want to launch English learners into academic success while maintaining and valuing the language they speak at home. Paired bilingual models immerse children in both English reading and native language reading at the same time. They are essentially half of a two-way bilingual model; by encouraging English proficient students to also take Spanish reading, any school with a paired bilingual model, according to the researchers, can readily become a two-way program, offering English-only children a path to early acquisition of a valuable second language.

Regardless of which school of thought one subscribes to, the role of oral language development in literacy is not to be discounted. Oral English language proficiency plays a major role in children's ability to read in English. The acquisition of oral English proficiency has been found to be a gradual process for English learners, with researchers such as Hakuta, Butler, and Witt (1999) arguing that it can take 3 to 5 years to develop, and academic English proficiency (defined by student performance on a variety of standardized English reading tests) can take 4 to 7 years.

In addressing the role of oral language development in literacy, Olsen (2010a) advises making the distinction between language development and literacy development. The researcher advocates that it is not sufficient to teach reading skills alone to English learners; extensive oral English language development must be incorporated into successful literacy instruction. In summary, second language literacy is characterized by two prominent factors that merit consideration by the reform-minded leader: the use of native language in literacy and the role of oral language development in literacy development.

Leadership Compass

The interplay between oral language development and English learner literacy is clear. Callahan (2006) suggests that programs focused solely on reading at the expense of English language development are insufficient for supporting the academic success of English learners. The researcher compared the effects of a reading intervention, in lieu of traditional English language development, on English learner achievement in a California high school. The study found a decrease in the California Standards Test (CST) scores among English learners who received the reading intervention in place of the English language development curriculum. English learners who received the English language development curriculum posted significantly higher CST Language Arts scores than students in the reading intervention group.

This insight poses implications for the reform-minded leader interested in addressing English learner literacy in his or her site. Short and Fitzsimmons (2007) offer an array of considerations for policymakers who want to improve English learner literacy. Among these considerations are: direct teaching of the components and processes of reading and writing, emphasizing reading comprehension strategies, focusing on vocabulary development, and using native language strategically. Therefore, school leaders considering an English learner literacy strategy should advocate for an initial focus on literacy that features elements of phonics, oral language, shared books, guided and independent reading, daily writing, and independent writing (Supovitz & Poglinco, 2001).

Test Your Knowledge

The development of second language literacy in schools merits special consideration by leaders interested in addressing the English learner literacy challenge. The complexity and factors that lead to developing reading skills in non–English learners are similar to those in English learners. Consider the following questions in examining second language literacy in your school:

1. What type of accommodations, if any, are made for English learners in developing literacy skills?
2. Are English learners taught reading skills in their native language? If so, how effective is this approach? If not, why?
3. How do your teachers use the development of English oral language proficiency to enhance the reading skills of English learners?

LITERACY BUILDING BLOCKS

Edvantia (2007) examined the seminal research effort by the National Reading Panel identifying five components essential for effective reading instruction: phonics, phonemic awareness, reading fluency, vocabulary, and reading comprehension. The panel's work, however, did not address research on the development of language and literacy among English learners. In addressing the void, the National Literacy Panel on Language-Minority Children and Youth subsequently examined the five components of reading from the English learner perspective and identified research that found that English learners can benefit from instruction focused on the five components—if such instruction embeds accommodations to meet the specific needs of English learners (August & Shanahan, 2006 as cited in Edvantia, 2007). The literacy building blocks of phonics, phonemic awareness, reading, fluency, vocabulary, and comprehension are critical in addressing what is known about developing English literacy in English learners (August, 2003).

Figure 7.1 provides a conceptual view of these components that help produce a fundamental understanding of the literacy building blocks. August (2003) emphasizes that phonics refers to the sounds of a language and how learners put sounds together to form words. Scaffolding on this concept, phonemic awareness is the ability to focus on and manipulate phonemes, the smallest units of spoken language. Phonemic awareness measured at the beginning of kindergarten is one of the best predictors of how well children are likely to learn to read. Reading fluency, on the other hand, is the ability to read text quickly, accurately, and with proper expression. Fluency may also extend beyond word recognition and incorporate the comprehension process as well (Thurlow & van den Broek, 1997, as cited in August, 2003). Next comes the important role that vocabulary plays in English learner literacy development. A major determinant of reading comprehension is vocabulary. Cunningham and Stanovich (1997) reported that

Figure 7.1. Literacy Building Blocks

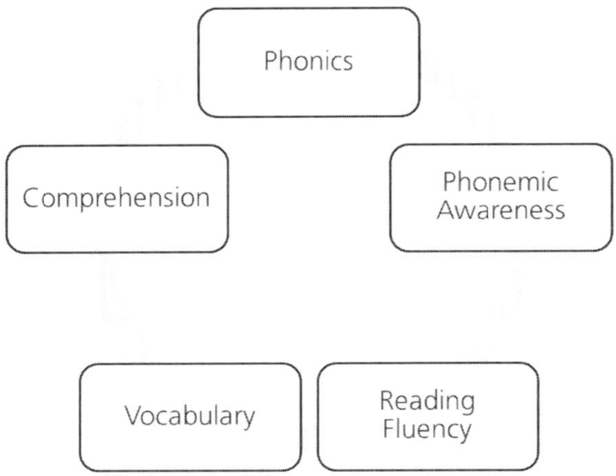

vocabulary assessed in 1st grade predicted more than 30% of reading comprehension variance in 11th grade. Finally, comprehension is seen not as a passive, receptive process, but as intentional thinking during which meaning is constructed through interactions with text and reader (August, 2003). A leader considering an English learner literacy strategy does well to consider and incorporate these components into the approach.

August and Shanahan (2006) argue for providing direct instruction on the components of reading: beginning with phonics and phonemic awareness and scaffolding into vocabulary, text comprehension, and fluency for English learners who do not read or write in any language and are beginning the path to literacy development. This instruction, the researchers argue, can focus on the English learner's native language or English. These components will readily transfer to English if they are taught in the native language. Teachers, however, should be cognizant and attentive to the differences between the native language and English. The researchers bring to the forefront that English has some phonemes that do not exist in other languages, such as the phoneme "sh," which does not occur in Spanish.

In addition to learning the basics of reading, Bernhardt (cited in Short & Fitzsimmons, 2007) advocates for English learners needing to receive explicit instruction on reading comprehension strategies. The transferability of the strategies to English will occur if the English learners already apply these strategies when reading in their native language. English learners, according to the researcher, need explicit instruction in strategy use in order to make the transfer. For adolescent English learners who lack reading strategies in their native language—for example, second language strategies—instruction can provide them with skills they can apply to all texts.

Leadership Compass

National, state, and regional education reforms continue to pressure schools to demonstrate increased student achievement inclusive of English learners. In response to these external reform demands, more and more school leaders are considering the role of literacy coaches in bringing about much-needed reform (Mangin, 2009) particularly in addressing English learners' literacy needs.

Hallinger (2003) calls for the reexamination of the principal leadership role by questioning what it means to be an instructional leader in the context of a reform initiative such as a literacy-coaching program. Much of the school leadership research literature defines principals' instructional leadership in terms of general behaviors and characteristics such as creating and sustaining professional development for teachers, fostering trust in schools, and providing resources for teachers and students.

The role of a literacy coach offers potent implications for enhancing an English learner literacy strategy. Mangin (2009) examined an approach for improving instruction through the development of instructional teacher leader roles also referred to as instructional coaches. These school-based, nonsupervisory roles are intended to be an on-site resource for teachers. Although there is no known research that demonstrates a causal link between instructional teacher leader roles and student achievement, the development of these roles is predicated on their potential for facilitating effective professional development. By providing sustained and context-specific professional development to teachers, instructional teacher leaders can improve instruction and thereby increase student achievement particularly in the literacy development of English learners. Based on this potential benefit, according to the researcher, instructional teacher leader roles have become a core component of large-scale school improvement initiatives.

Matsumura, Sartoris, Bickel, and Garnier (2009) suggest that leaders' actions and their beliefs regarding the roles and responsibilities of a coach play an important role in the implementation of coaching in schools. In an evaluation of a districtwide literacy coach initiative, for example, Camburn, Kimball, and Lowenhaupt (2008, as cited in Matsumura et al., 2009) found that coaches and the district administrators overseeing their work reported that principals' demands on coaches to perform administrative and managerial tasks was a significant impediment to their work with teachers. These teacher leaders or coaches reported that lack of content expertise on the part of coaches made teachers less likely to participate in coaching.

Armed with this knowledge base, how is the school leader to address the English learner literacy issue in his or her school? Whether at the elementary or secondary level, the role of peer coaching on literacy development merits consideration. One such effective model is literacy coaching. When carefully conceptualized and crafted, the literacy coach function can have a profound impact on English learner literacy development. For school leaders interested in helping teachers embrace literacy development for English learners, this model holds promise.

Test Your Knowledge

A coherent English learner literacy strategy incorporates the essential components for effective reading instruction: phonics, phonemic awareness, fluency, vocabulary, and comprehension. These literacy building blocks ensure that no English learner falls through the cracks in literacy development. In this context, reflect on the following questions:

1. How do your teachers assess reading fluency and comprehension in English learners?
2. Is there direct instruction for English learners in these literacy components?
3. How would a literacy coach be beneficial to the English learners in your school?

SUSTAINABILITY INDICATOR: TEACHER RETENTION

English learners attend schools characterized by low academic performance as well as high poverty rates. In addition to these two significant traits is high teacher turnover. A reform-minded leader who is investing time and resources in English learner literacy must also contend with the challenge of teacher retention. While schools have the responsibility to provide effective and ongoing training on literacy development for its teaching force, the next challenge for leaders is how to retain trained teachers. Hence, one of the most critical components of sustaining literacy reform efforts is teacher retention. Teacher retention is a problem in public schools that can and should be addressed if school reform is to be sustained.

Planty et al. (2008) found that at the end of the 2003–2004 school year, 17% of the elementary and secondary teacher workforce in their study left the public and private schools where they had been teaching. Although this turnover is inclusive of teachers transferring to another school, the implications of teacher retention on reform sustainability are enormous.

Carroll and Fulton (2004) assert that the top reasons for teachers leaving the profession were lack of professional support, poor school leadership, low pay, and personal reasons. In their study examining reasons why teachers leave the profession, Tye and O'Brien (2002) concluded that among the major reasons cited by teachers were accountability, increased paperwork, student attitudes, no parent support, and low status of the profession. Apparently, it was the work environment itself that ultimately proved unbearable, and the pressures connected to standardized testing were a prominent feature of that work environment. The researchers argue that conditions that undermine the power and effectiveness of the public school system need to be identified and promptly rectified. This includes, above all, creating a work environment that will continue to draw the bright, committed new teachers U.S. schools need—and that will keep them enthusiastic, energetic, and productive throughout their careers.

Tending to a positive work environment as a teacher retention tool, Van Houtte (2006) contends, leads to an increase in job satisfaction. In past decades, researchers have devoted much study to determine job satisfaction in various professions, including the teaching profession. Low job satisfaction has been associated with stress, burnout, lack of commitment to the institution, absenteeism, and turnover issues that clearly make it desirable to better understand the factors that influence satisfaction.

Renzulli, Parrott, and Beattie (2011) argue that dissatisfaction and job turnover among teachers impact not only individual teachers' careers but also the broader school community. In their study examining the effects of racial mismatch on teacher satisfaction and subsequent turnover, the researchers found that teaching in racially mismatched schools results in lower levels of satisfaction for White teachers. Their work has shown that teacher satisfaction is related to both the racial composition and the organizational structure of the schools in which teachers work. This significant piece of work poses tremendous implications for this country's public school system given that the diversity of its teaching force is not keeping up with the diversity of its student population.

Summing up the important role of teacher retention in sustaining school reform efforts, Coggins, Zuckerman, and McKelvey (2011) argue that leaders interested in narrowing the achievement gap should retain effective teachers and make them available for those children on the losing side of the gap.

The rubric shown in Table 7.2 is provided as a tool for school leaders to dialogue with staff on their school's progress in English learner programming.

Table 7.2. Coherent Literacy Strategy

Element of English Learner Programming	Emerging Stage	Developing Stage	Sustainability Stage
Confronting the English Learner Literacy Challenges	EL literacy is not addressed by the school staff. There is little or no interest in identifying the reading levels of ELs undergirded by a fight-or-flight attitude. English learner literacy is perceived as someone else's responsibility.	The school takes steps to address the literacy challenges faced by ELs by making efforts to analyze data on EL reading levels. Struggling EL readers have been identified and are provided interventions to address their literacy needs. When appropriate, efforts are made to provide reading instruction in the ELs' first language.	The school staff takes ownership of the literacy challenges faced by ELs. Staff members view the ELs' learning and academic literacy development as their responsibility. The reading levels of all the ELs in the school have been identified and specific interventions for struggling readers are provided. Mainstream teachers understand and promote their role in helping develop literacy skills in ELs.
Second Language Literacy	The school has not provided any professional development for teachers on second language literacy. There has been little or no effort to establish a common understanding of the complexity of the reading process for ELs. Teachers are not expected to develop second language literacy in their ELs.	There is some schoolwide effort to review and address the second language literacy needs of ELs. Discussions are being held on understanding the distinction between language development and literacy development. Limited professional development on the strategic use of native language in literacy development has been provided to teachers.	Teachers work in collaborative teams to develop shared knowledge on the complexities of second language literacy. EL literacy expectations from grade level to grade level are clearly articulated. Teachers understand the interplay between oral language development and EL literacy and are committed to instructing their students in the essential learning in second language literacy.
Literacy Building Blocks	Teachers are unfamiliar with the literacy building blocks and tend to blame the sending school for the ELs' literacy needs. There is little or no effort to address EL literacy needs. There is no evidence of direct instruction on the literacy building blocks in the classroom.	Some teachers of the same grade level or department are discussing means to address vocabulary scaffolding, text comprehension, and fluency for ELs. Explicit instruction on the literacy building blocks varies from teacher to teacher, with EL accommodations evident in some classrooms.	There is a collective inquiry in the school about the use of the literacy building blocks to address EL reading needs. Teachers are well versed on the literacy building blocks with professional development provided to sustain the shared knowledge. There is evidence of direct instruction in the components of literacy development in all classrooms.

Chapter 7 Application Exercises:
Coherent Literacy Strategy: Gateway to English Learner Academic Success

Individual Exercise This chapter has highlighted that many teachers, both at the elementary as well as the secondary level, are not trained or versed in literacy development in general and much less for English learners. If this scenario is manifested in your school, how would you plan to begin hosting dialogues on English learner literacy development? Many teachers do not see themselves as responsible for developing literacy skills in English learners on top of teaching content. How would you begin disrupting this belief system in teachers?

Team Exercise Prepare a list of all your English learners by grade level in your schools. With the help of a data analyst, examine the reading levels of each of the English learners on your list. What percent of your English learners are reading at grade level? What percent are reading below grade level? Share these findings with your teachers at your next grade-level, department, or leadership team meeting by posing the following questions: How do these literacy rates impact the academic achievement of English learners? How should we as school leaders address this issue?

School Exercise In an effort to make the English learner literacy challenge transparent in your school, share the English learner reading-level data from the previous exercise at your next schoolwide meeting. Provide copies of Figure 7.2 for all teachers and remind them that researchers August and Shanahan (2006) argue that direct instruction on these literacy building blocks is essential for English learner literacy development. In tables of job-alike groups, have your teams respond to the following questions: Which component of the model poses the greatest challenge for English learners in your classroom? Why? After 15 minutes, ask for a whole-group debriefing and tabulate the responses on chart paper. After all groups have reported, ask the group how a coherent literacy strategy for English learners might be structured in your school. Encourage lively dialogue.

8

Building School Capacity for English Learner Success

Avoiding the Permanent Dead-End

> *Long-term observers of educational innovation and school reform have argued that reform might more productively be seen as a problem of learning than as a problem of implementation. That is, the progress of reform appears to rest in crucial ways on the capacity of teachers, both individually and collectively. (Little, 1999, p. 2)*

Mintrop (2004) asserts that high-stakes accountability reforms cannot realize their stated aims unless targeted schools can develop the capacity to meet prescribed performance standards. After a track record of unsuccessful reform efforts, researchers and reformers argue that public school districts are dysfunctional institutions that lack the capacity to implement much-needed improvements, and, in fact, often obstruct needed reforms (Hess, 1999). Although this criticism has been aimed at large, urban school systems, critics contend that many of the nation's schools are ineffective bureaucracies (Corcoran & Lawrence, 2003). For reforms to succeed, Firestone (1989) chimes in, districts must have the will to change, which, when coupled with capacity building, can lead to effective reform in schools.

The dissatisfaction with America's schools has led to demands for systemic change throughout the K–12 systems, including changes in district functioning and schoolwide practices, as well as in the classroom. In the midst of this dissatisfaction with schools is a prevalent view that many of today's educational leaders lack the skill set to lead such changes (Brown, Stroh, Fouts, & Baker, 2005).

In recent years, key lessons have emerged in the literature, leading to a clearer understanding of how districts implement reform and how these systems build school capacity and improve student learning (Fullan, Bertani,

& Quinn, 2004). Many of the attributes of effective reforms impact English learner achievement. Factors that can contribute to the success of English learners include schoolwide commitment to English learner achievement, consistent language support services of adequate duration across all grade levels, sufficient educator capacity, and a match between resources and the community served (Edvantia, 2007).

As the preceding chapter highlighted, teachers have little or no training in helping English learners develop second language literacy to successfully master content-area material. Francis, Rivera, Lesaux, Keiffer, and Rivera (2006) reveal that teachers need sustained, job-embedded professional development in helping English learners understand not only course content but also the academic language used to learn the content. Those who receive such training gain an arsenal of instructional techniques that can help not only English learners, but also native English speakers, especially low-performing students.

Developing school capacity for English learner reform requires more than providing professional development for teachers. Cohen and Ball (1996) propose an expansive view of school capacity where, in addition to teachers' knowledge and skill development, school capacity should encompass high-quality instructional materials and students and teachers who are motivated and ready to learn. Goertz, Floden, and O'Day (1995) describe dimensions of school capacity that include access to knowledge, school structure and resources, and leadership. Sipple and Killeen (2004) suggest that school capacity, which includes teachers' professional knowledge and skills, financial resources, and specifically effective leadership at the district and building levels, is important for increasing a school's ability to deliver high-quality instruction—in this case, more so for English learner academic success.

In their attempts to further the understanding of the concept of school capacity, policymakers, researchers, and practitioners alike have identified a plethora of characteristics. Corcoran and Goertz (1995) argue that the key components of building school capacity fall into three categories: (1) the intellectual ability, knowledge, and skills of teachers and other staff; (2) the quality and quantity of the resources available for teaching, including staffing levels, instructional time, and class sizes; and (3) the social organization of instruction or instructional culture. Others researchers, such as Youngs and King (2002), employ different categories and labels, such as human, financial, and technical resources, or include program coherence and organizational coordination as elements of capacity building in schools. Similarly, Malen and Rice (2004) developed a framework that includes both a resource dimension and a productivity dimension to building capacity in schools. They argue that this dual-dimensional construction of school capacity encourages a more complete exploration of the manner in which education reform policies might alter school capacity.

At the epicenter of this vast array of attributes resides leadership. Sipple and Killeen (2004) suggest that effective leadership at the district and building levels is important for increasing an organization's ability to deliver high-quality instruction. Although the definition of school capacity may vary from researcher to researcher, the role of the school leader is a common denominator that is either explicitly or implicitly factored into this concept. Figure 8.1 illustrates a conceptual model for thinking about school capacity with leadership at its core.

Borrowing from the work of Corcoran and Goertz (1995), who identified key components of capacity building, this chapter navigates through a conceptual understanding of building school capacity for English learner reform through a call for the school leader to focus on three critical dimensions:

- Intellectual capacity;
- Resource utility; and
- Organizational development.

Figure 8.1. Elements of School Capacity

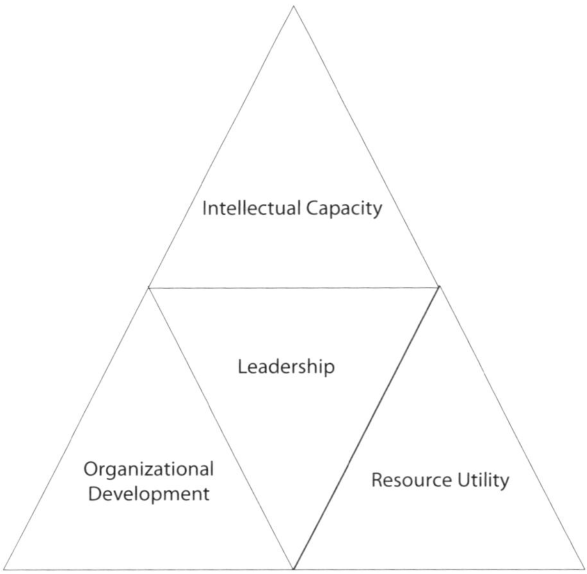

Additionally, a discussion ensues on how leadership undergirds these three dimensions, both individually and collectively. Culminating this chapter is the sustainability framework indicator by the same name as a means of deepening an understanding of this important concept.

INTELLECTUAL CAPACITY

Unless reform efforts infiltrate the classroom, where English learners are struggling to simultaneously learn English as well as content, the chance of narrowing the achievement gap is slim. Developing and sustaining teacher knowledge and skills is essential to all reform efforts, but more so for English learner reform. Biancarosa and Snow (2004) write that many of the educators working in this nation's public schools have had little professional development for teaching English learners. This lack of adequate teacher development conflicts with the fact that the relationship between literacy proficiency and academic achievement grows stronger as grade levels rise—regardless of individual student characteristics. English learners, therefore, need teachers skillful in each content area who can help them develop their second language as they simultaneously learn, comprehend, and apply content-area concepts through that second language. Stated differently, the intellectual capacity of a teaching force is contingent on the effort put forth to develop the skill set of these teachers. Administrators can support schoolwide commitment to English learner achievement by securing high-quality staff development and providing opportunities for collaboration among subject-area teachers (Short & Fitzsimmons, 2007).

Building the intellectual capacity of staff for English learner reform requires targeted and sustained professional development. Park and Datnow (2008) recall that over the past decade, the definition of effective professional development for educators has evolved into one that emphasizes situated learning rather than discrete training sessions removed from the day-to-day needs of the classroom. Situated learning, the researchers declare, focuses on context-specific learning opportunities whereby teachers within a school relate to one another as peer coaches and as learners in a community. These learning opportunities yield relationships in schools that are often defined in terms of collaboration, reciprocity, and mutual engagement in developing reflective instructional practices.

Kruse (2008) maintains that how schools transform and how professional development is addressed ultimately influence the success or failure of school reforms. Although efforts to improve teaching and learning are at the core of school reform, such programs are impaired by mitigating factors such as poorly implemented reforms, limited capacity to foster professional learning, and fragmented distributed leadership that inhibits schoolwide change. The researcher suggests that reforming schools must address their work by building on assets, challenging deeply held assumptions about student learning and providing for organizational improvement.

Without question, an integral aspect of developing intellectual capacity for learning and school improvement is driven by the quality of professional development. The traditional one-shot training sessions do little to address the specific needs of schools, and teachers cannot support the ongoing learning that is required for capacity building. Park and Datnow (2008) contend that effective professional development is characterized by opportunities where teachers share, discuss, and apply what they are learning with other practitioners. For this type of professional development and collaboration to occur, system-level support needs to be in place. In addition to consistent structured time for collaboration and professional learning, schools need strategies for planning, sharing, and evaluating their efforts. This coordination of human, social, material, and technical resources contribute to capacity-building efforts.

Leadership Compass

Embedded within the element of school capacity is the notion of collaboration. English learner reform requires a collaborative team approach that seeks continuous improvement. Teams working together develop clear, operational understandings of their goals and strategies, fostering new ideas, skills, and a shared commitment to schoolwide improvement (Fullan et al., 2004). The reform-minded leader develops intellectual capacity by providing effective professional development as well as establishing a collaborative work environment. Slater (2008) claims that the success of a school leader's performance is determined by his or her ability to inspire a culture of empowerment by acting as a hero-maker rather than a hero. Leveraging the resources of others is essential for the site-based breakthroughs or changes in complex school systems and in turn builds human capacity and self-knowledge. In order to develop human potential, the researcher advises, the leader needs to know people well, look for strengths in individuals, and build upon them. Effective communication is instrumental in establishing collaborative relationships and is a key aspect of building intellectual capacity in a school. These relationships provide the framework within which people come to understand and value each other's experiences, interests, and dreams.

Reitzug, West, and Angel (2008) suggest that through a focus on building personal relationships with teachers and students, principals who ground their work in the relationships of schools focus their attentions on developing school cultures that foster positive attitudes toward change and improvement.

Relationship building in the context of developing intellectual capacity of staff is essential for English learner reform. Copland (2003) points out that the history of school reform offers a striking contrast regarding the efficacy of such an approach to leadership for widespread improvement in America's public schools. What history shows is that the traditional hierarchical model of school leadership, in which identified leaders in positions of formal authority make critical improvement decisions and then seek, through various strategies, to promote adherence to those decisions among those who occupy the rungs of the ladder below, has failed to adequately answer repeated calls for sweeping educational improvements across American schools.

This relationship building empowers teachers to take ownership of English learners in their classrooms. Relationship building additionally calls for the leader's ability to capture the energy of people by capitalizing on the various leadership attributes of school members.

Test Your Knowledge

A collaborative work environment is a pathway to building relationships with teachers who engender a trust level where lack of skill sets to address English learner needs are discussed without fear of repercussions. Reflect on your school's environment and respond to the following questions:

1. What role does your school environment play in developing the intellectual capacity of your staff?
2. Describe the connection between your professional relationship with teachers and the level of trust among colleagues in your schools.
3. What evidence can you produce to illustrate the impact that your leadership has had on developing the intellect of your teaching force?

RESOURCE UTILITY

The second dimension of building school capacity encompasses an examination of fiscal, material, informational, and productivity aspects of capacity building. Crowson and Boyd (1992) argue that school systems are unable to adequately cope with reforms due to financial and organizational constraints. In their study of the role of fiscal capital in school reform, Malen and Rice (2004) found that during the initial year of reform, Title I schools received relatively modest but direct financial allocations to support their school improvement initiatives. However, the size and duration of these initial, single-shot allocations left the schools heavily dependent on their Title I supplements and on their ability to compete for so-called soft monies. These schools were not granted a competitive advantage in bids for access to additional discretionary funds.

Although some politicians, and some educators for that matter, may argue that the increasing of resources is not the solution to addressing low English learner performance in the nation's public schools, Lesaux, Kieffer, Faller, and Kelley (2010) insist that resources are essential to building school capacity. In their study of the impact of resources on program implementation, the researchers concluded that program resources/materials indeed matter. The need and use of curricular materials were discussed repeatedly in the teacher logs and the interviews examined by the researchers. The curriculum was perceived as the essential component of support in a reform. The majority of teachers interviewed in the study described the materials as highly supportive.

The role of resource provision in building capacity in schools, however, extends beyond the fiscal allocations or material allotments. How the resources are utilized has a direct bearing on capacity building. The alignment of internal resources plays an important role in ensuring that the proper resources are provided for addressing the academic needs of English learners. In their work examining linear instructional leaders, Reitzug et al. (2008) advocate for a leader's focus on the shared work of standards and curriculum alignment, data collection and analysis, and problem-based decision-making. By continuously aligning the standards–instruction–assessment cycle, these instructional leaders focus their attention on what they believe to be the most direct path to improvement. In the case of English learner programming, this type of instructional leadership would ensure, first and foremost, that English learners are provided equal access to core curriculum, eliminating the chance of any semblance of tracking. This type of linear leadership will additionally ensure that English learner assessment data (English language proficiency and content mastery) are used to modify instruction in the classroom so that English learners are meeting mainstream standards.

A different way of looking at internal resources and their role in capacity building is through the lens of productivity. Here, school capacity is viewed beyond the resources available to a school. Instead, this perspective advocates for the maximum amount of production that can be obtained from a given set of resources and organizational arrangements (Corcoran & Goertz, 1995, as cited in Malen & Rice, 2004). In other words, this dimension of capacity building, takes into account the ability of a school to translate resources into expected outcomes.

Another perspective in examining the role of resources in building school capacity for English learner reform success is through informational resources. Informational resources, according to Malen and Rice (2004), refer to opportunities for principals and teachers to acquire new ideas and examine the consequences of their actions. These opportunities are often procured through various forms of professional development, including opportunities to learn from practice. Indicators include informal information channels, such as spontaneous conversations with colleagues, as well as evaluative practices that occur as a direct or indirect result of a given reform. Assuming a slightly different twist, this factor is closely linked to the professional development dimension of capacity building.

While much of the discussion on the role of resources in capacity building has been focused at the school level, the role of the district is not to be discounted. Sipple and Killeen (2004) assert that districts remain the legal and fiscal agents responsible for carrying out states' educational obligations and are the major source of capacity building for schools and teachers. Districts are the conduits for providing and controlling access to data, strengthening professional development opportunities, guiding curricular and instructional initiatives, and fostering relationships with external agents. Consequently, as policymakers attempt to align state instructional policy to provide more coherent guidance for classroom teachers in support of ambitious learning outcomes, district responses to these initiatives must be considered.

Leadership Compass

The effective and efficient use of resources in capacity building requires leaders to continuously develop coalitions. Failed reforms in the past have taught us the harsh lesson that schools do not function in isolation. Walker and Gutmore (2001) divulge that policy responses to comprehensive reform initiatives necessitate the creation of cross-sector coalitions to support change. The researchers investigated the factors that successfully predict districts' abilities to generate cross-sector support for reforms. Their study explored the extent to which the level of support generated within district communities impacts their willingness to embrace the support reforms and their perspectives of resource problems. The researchers argue that assumptions about successful urban school transformation must be predicated on the understanding that urban schools, like all other formal institutions, are influenced by the intersection of several forces: political, economic, racial, and sociocultural differences. The researchers contend that if the current reforms are to be sustainable over time, then attention must be paid to the development of communitywide support in a form that is coherent and focused. Their work concluded that reforms and policy environments must be redefined to align with the realities of urban schooling.

While the public school reform agenda continues to be dominated by the call for the involvement of all community constituencies, Walker and Gutmore (2001) warn that community involvement in the current reform is characterized by the peripheral support of corporate, foundation, political, and religious segments. The involvement in school reform in reality comes from school boards, teachers' unions, parents, and community-based organizations. The researchers caution that there are challenges in involving non-educators in educational problem-solving. The history of failed reforms, coupled with the unstable reform environment that exemplifies many schools, renders coalition building difficult. The sheer magnitude of current reforms will require the support of various groups if they are to be successful. Civic capacity must be considered in order to mitigate against the sense of isolation that districts experience from key civic groups' noninvolvement in reform efforts. This is of particular importance, as civic groups have the potential to contribute valuable resources to change efforts (Walker & Gutmore, 2001).

In instituting reform aimed at narrowing the English learner achievement gap, the leader must tend to these cross-sector coalitions both internally and externally. In addressing internal coalitions, Fullan et al. (2004) advocate for lateral capacity building that encompasses outreaching and connecting to schools within a district to develop new ideas and skills, and to share promising practices that increase the ability of individuals and organizations to bring about improvement. The researchers highlight an example of lateral capacity building in England where the district leadership and principals paired schools and departments to raise the bar and close the achievement gap. A group of math teachers who have been successful in motivating otherwise disengaged students' work with teachers in another math department who are dealing with similar problems without much success. This new way of learning is a feature of building capacity in schools and school districts. When done well, these efforts have considerable benefits. Individual school principals become almost as concerned about the success of other schools in the district as they are about their own. Teams working together develop clear, operational understandings of their goals and strategies, fostering new ideas and skills, and a shared commitment to districtwide improvement (Fullan et al., 2004). In the context of resource utility, coalition building is becoming more of a necessity to facilitate the building of school capacity for English learner reform.

Test Your Knowledge

Budget constraints have had an adverse effect on school reform. In many cases, reform efforts have been suspended while tending to, what in many cases is, the sheer survival of schools. As you examine resource utility in your school, address the following questions:

1. How do you reconcile the need for sustaining English learner reform with the dwindling of resources?
2. What efforts have you taken to leverage or align the resources in hand to push for addressing the academic needs of English learners?
3. How would you use your teachers' collective expertise to build cross-sector coalitions to support English learner needs?

ORGANIZATIONAL DEVELOPMENT

Massell (1998) contends that over the last decade or more, the architecture of reform has been the focus of policymakers. Performance standards, standardized tests, and accountability systems contributed to the formation of this architecture. With the infrastructure in place, attention can now be given to building the capacity needed to achieve higher standards. Policy analysts have used the idea of capacity to explain why simply having clear ideas about learning goals or high motivation does not always yield the hoped-for learning in students. Many states with high standards, assessments, and accountability programs are finding that early gains in student achievement have reached a plateau, and that gaps between poor, non-poor, majority, and minority student achievement persist.

Capacity building, according to Brown et al. (2005), calls for going beyond the development of intellectual capacity and resource utility to simultaneously address the organizational needs of a school. Tending to the organizational structure, the researchers write, involves addressing adult perspectives and beliefs about all aspects of the educational experience, including an understanding about the need for change, the process of change, beliefs about student capabilities, and effective teaching practices. The attention given to capacity-building efforts, at least initially, has been focused on the district and building administrators have been charged with leading this process.

It is the school leader's responsibility to develop the school as a whole as a readiness effort for English learner reform. Brown et al. (2005) state that as the nation's schools are attempting to meet the accountability demands, educators are investigating ways to effectively change the organizations responsible for student learning. Reform-minded leaders are realizing that the very nature of the organization itself must be changed if students are to meet the new learning expectations. The American public school system, with its extended history of tradition, will require impacting the underlying beliefs and values that are the basis for current practices. Past reform efforts have failed to recognize that impacting these beliefs and values will require considerable adult learning for educators before meaningful modifications in school environments and teaching and learning can take place, given the political undercurrents of the English learner issue. The challenge faced by reformers is to find the most effective way to create a comprehensive adult learning environment, something that does not exist in many American schools.

To address these fundamental belief systems and social structures in schools, Reitzug et al. (2008) suggest an organic approach to leadership practice. The organic leader presumes that instructional components cannot be addressed in isolation from the larger school organization. From this perspective, the organic leader takes in the wider school culture in accounting for instructional leadership efforts. Organic leaders, according to the researchers, use a variety of structural, political, and human resource forms to stimulate discussion, shared work, and problem-solving contributing to developing the organizational culture of a school. When it comes to English learners, organic leaders ensure that the school culture embraces and owns up to addressing the needs of English learners. This type of leadership focuses on unveiling the belief systems behind English learner challenges being faced by staff. This practice unearths a school's collective attitude toward English learner potential, teacher expectations of English learners, and most important, English learner access to core curriculum.

As tax-supported institutions, the social structure of schools is influenced by external factors—particularly political forces. As the previous section showed, developing cross-sector support for educational reform points to some of the inherent difficulties with the process. Walker and Gutmore (2001) argue that race and class cleavages and their intersections can create internal ripple effects and impact belief systems. Stone (2001, as cited in Walker & Gutmore, 2001) points out cases in Atlanta, St. Louis, Baltimore, and El Paso in which civic groups were unable to coalesce around educational reform because of racial differences. The researcher found that during the early 1990s in Atlanta, racial tension, both inside and outside the educational system, precluded the development of any communitywide cooperation around educational issues. So, in tending to the social structure of schools, it behooves leaders to consider the internal factors, such as belief systems in the guise of teacher expectations, as well as the external forces, such as political and racial undertones.

Leadership Compass

Slater (2008) contends that leadership behavior that attends to the school culture nurtures the empowerment and capacity of other individuals in the school. The behavior of leaders, according to the researcher, has a major impact on people. The reform-minded leader is charged with creating an environment that unleashes the creativity and energy of people and that motivates them to contribute.

These leadership behaviors may also require leaders to function as servants to the school organization, its students and teachers, and its visions and values. These prophetic leaders focus on identifying what might be and establish practices, programs, and policies designed to inspire school leaders to use their positional power to reorient school personnel to the broader purposes of education, schools, and schooling (Reitzug et al., 2008). Prophetic instructional leaders ensure that staff serving English learners realize the moral and ethical responsibilities required to work in these schools. This type of leadership assumes responsibility for every student, providing English learners with an opportunity to excel in school.

Soliciting the objectivity of an external perspective is a critical element in minding to the school culture. Park and Datnow (2008) examined the role of external service providers in capacity building. The researchers analyzed the impact of the Success for All Foundation (SFAF)—the nonprofit intermediary organization that promotes Success for All (SFA). This organization works with educators in schools to increase capacity for learning and instruction. Success for All is a comprehensive school-reform model that primarily centers on early literacy intervention. Building on research of intermediary organizations, the researchers observed how SFAF structures professional development and the types of relationships the organization cultivates with practitioners. The researchers concluded that this external provider, in essence, assumes the role of capacity coach.

Brown et al. (2005) advocate for the notion of capacity coaches in developing the school as an organization. Capacity coaches have become popular as attempts to change or reinvent the entire organization have increased. In either a changing or reinventing role, effective capacity coaches must be knowledgeable about all matters in education, including school policy, instructional strategies, and curriculum, and must be able to establish honest and trusting relationships with their staff.

Test Your Knowledge

The development of the school as an organization is of critical importance in capacity building. This complex charge calls for a leader to be cognizant of the change process. As you examine your school from a systemic perspective, reflect on the following questions:

1. How have your professional development efforts impacted the belief systems and attitudes of your teachers toward English learners?
2. Describe the collective attitude of your teachers toward English learners.
3. Can you identify any political or racial undertones that may be playing a role in this collective attitude?

SUSTAINABILITY INDICATOR: SCHOOL CAPACITY

There is an interesting double entendre prevailing through this chapter focusing on capacity building. School capacity must be built to allow for English learner reform to flourish. School capacity must also be sustained to institutionalize the same English learner reform. In looking at capacity building as a sustainability indicator, Hoshchild (2003) warns that the fate of any education reform is contingent on the capacity of schools to do what the policy expects or requires in light of the fact that high-stakes accountability policies impose ambitious demands and stiff sanctions on schools. Hence, the impact of these accountability policies on the capacity of schools to improve their performance warrants special attention. Goertz et al. (1995) argue that successful reform, in particular the positive effects of standards-based reform policies on instruction, depends on the capacities of the organizations (schools, districts, and states) that surround the classroom. The building of school capacity is an essential element in building and sustaining English learner reform.

In a 5-year impact study, Parrish, Perez, Merickel, and Linquanti (2006) examined the schools that were most successful with English learners and identified three common factors: (1) staff with the training and capabilities to address English learners' linguistic and cognitive needs, (2) a schoolwide focus on English language development, and (3) data-driven instruction.

Capacity building in schools comes in many forms. Johnson, Hays, Center, and Daley's (2004) study of school reform found a number of capacity-building factors (i.e., type of structure and formal linkages, presence of champions for an innovation, effective leadership, resources, administrative policies and procedures, and expertise) that need to be addressed to sustain innovations. There are also known causal factors, which are attributes or characteristics of an innovation that heighten its potential to be sustained. These innovation attributes include alignment with needs, positive relationships among stakeholders, and ownership by implementers.

Borko, Wolf, Simone, and Uchiyama (2003) studied two elementary schools, identified as exemplary by Washington educators, as they worked to enact Washington's Essential Academic Learning Requirements and help students achieve proficiency on the Washington Assessment of Student Learning. The researchers identified six dimensions of school capacity: principal leadership; professional community; program coherence; technical resources; knowledge, skills, and dispositions of individual teachers; and learning opportunities for teachers. Supporting the claim that school reform takes time, the researchers concluded that young reform efforts are best understood in terms of capacity building rather than outcome.

Capacity building has become a phrase used to acknowledge that clear standards and aligned assessments are not enough to dramatically change teaching and learning (Massell, 1998). The capacity needed for school reform remains poorly defined and not well understood. Many people tend to think primarily, and sometimes exclusively, of the need to improve teachers' knowledge and skills. However, the necessary capacities and strategies must be thought of more extensively and indeed more systemically.

This chapter has considered not only what is meant by school capacity but also how to build and sustain this elusive element of school reform. In addition to teachers' knowledge and skills, effective classrooms (which are the targets of reforms) require high-quality instructional materials and students and teachers who are motivated and ready to learn (Cohen & Ball, 1996). This chapter has also examined three broad dimensions of capacity building in schools for English learner success: intellectual capacity, resource utility, and organizational development. To ensure the sustainability of English learner reform, these three dimensions must be tended to simultaneously by the school leader. From a strategic point of view, capacity building encompasses going beyond short- or even mid-term results. Capacity building calls for particular attention to the sustainability of an infrastructure where English learner success is not left up to chance. Fullan et al. (2004) assert that ultimately, the main mark of successful leaders is not so much their impact on student learning at the end of their tenure, but rather the number of good leaders they leave behind who can go even further. These two aspects, according to the researchers, are not mutually exclusive; leaders need to focus on both achievement and the development of future leaders.

The rubric shown in Table 8.1 is provided as a tool for school leaders to dialogue with staff on their school's progress in English learner programming.

Table 8.1. Building School Capacity for English Learner Success

Element of English Learner Programming	Emerging Stage	Developing Stage	Sustainability Stage
Developing Intellectual Capacity	Developing teachers' knowledge and skills about EL academic needs is minimal or not addressed in the school. Teachers are expected to meet the day-to-day needs of ELs on their own. There is no established collaboration time for teachers to share learning experiences with each other.	The professional development focusing on EL issues is characterized by an occasional workshop. There is an effort to foster professional learning but the training sessions are fragmented, lacking cohesion. Much of the professional development for teachers is done in the traditional one-shot training that does not support ongoing learning for capacity building.	There is a schoolwide commitment to EL achievement evidenced by high-quality professional development supplemented with opportunities for collaboration among subject-area teachers. In the learning opportunities, teachers relate to one another as peer coaches and readily share, discuss, and apply what they are learning with each other.
Resource Utility	There are few or no resources available to teachers to address the academic needs of ELs. There is no budget allocated for teacher materials for use with ELs or for professional development. There is a lack of curriculum and supplemental resources for teachers to use to help develop English language proficiency with ELs.	While there are some ELD curriculum/ materials available for teachers, they are not sufficient to meet the needs of ELs. Teachers are expected to make accommodations for ELs based on limited supplemental materials. The internal resources of the school are not aligned for addressing the academic needs of ELs.	EL program resources/materials are readily available to teachers for instructional use with ELs in their classrooms. Budget allocations allow for teachers to attend conferences to expand their skill sets on meeting EL academic needs. The EL materials/curriculum are aligned to state and district standards. ELs are provided equal access to the curriculum.
Organizational Development	The status quo is pervasive in the school. There is no effort to address and develop adult learning as a means of modifying the school environment. An adult learning environment, where teaching and learning are given top priority, is nonexistent in the school. Staff lacks the motivation to be creative.	While some teachers may embrace the need for EL school reform, little is understood about the change process. Beliefs about EL capabilities and effective teaching practices are not articulated schoolwide. There are sporadic discussions about developing the organizational culture of the school, but for the most part, there is no systematic approach to building capacity.	The school culture allows for the challenging of deeply held assumptions about student learning. The school culture is defined by professional relationships that encourage reflective instructional practices. Adults in the school embrace the need for change in order to meet the academic needs of ELs. There is a clear schoolwide reform effort to address EL needs.

Chapter 8 Application Exercises:
Building School Capacity for English Learner Success

Individual Exercise Another way of looking at school capacity is through the building of shared knowledge among your staff. DuFour et al. (2004) argue that building shared knowledge is the way questions are answered and issues are resolved in schools. What is the single major EL issue that needs to be addressed in your school? How would you go about building shared knowledge in your school to address this single issue? How are you at aligning your resources to address this issue?

Team Exercise Immunity to change (Brown et al., 2005) is a phenomenon that can impede EL reform efforts. In diagnosing this concept, it is important to unearth teachers' competing commitments and uncover big assumptions for EL reform. At your next leadership team meeting, use a "four-column" exercise to have each member of your team identify his or her commitments and assumptions on EL reform. On chart paper, label the first column, "I am committed to . . ."; the second column, "What am I doing or not doing that is keeping my commitment from being fully realized?"; the third column, "Competing Commitments"; and finally, the fourth column, "Big Assumptions." Ask each member of your team to fill in each of the columns with their respective insights. Discuss the implications of your team's thoughts.

School Exercise At your next schoolwide meeting, distribute copies of Figure 8.1 to each of your teachers. Inform your staff that building capacity for EL success requires addressing all four dimensions on the graphic. Ask each table group to list the four dimensions in order of priority needed to address the academic needs of ELs in your school and to justify their priorities. Monitor the discussion. After 20 minutes, have each group report. Tabulate the various responses on chart paper. Discuss the variance in responses. Ask the whole group to reach consensus on which dimension should be focused on in moving forward with EL reform in your school.

9

A Comprehensive Model for English Learner Instructional Improvement

Mapping a Course of Action

> *It is time to recognize that weak programs and approaches are foreclosing life options for many students who struggle along, year to year, falling further and further behind. This is wholly reparable, and it is in our power to create policies and practices . . . and support for schools to address the needs of . . . English Learners.*
> *(Olsen, 2010a, p. 33)*

The fundamental claim in this book is that broad-based English learner school reform can be sustained. The common thread is the unwrapping of organizational structures and their accompanying leadership skills to ensure the sustainability of English learner reform. This work has consciously shied away from the provision of a cafeteria-style menu of English learner programs that could be considered for reform. Instead, this manuscript has focused on the examination of deeper fundamental school structures required to ensure English learner success, all the while guiding the school leader in handling the reform terrain deftly. The intention is quite simple: structural reform that has an outsize effect on the classroom.

The creation of enduring structures can be viewed through the three-pronged approach advocated by Confrey, Castro-Filho, and Wilhelm (2000). First, the researchers define school structures as the adequate channels for the delivery of effective services to students. Second, structure can also be seen as the organizational arrangements for the delivery of instruction along with the use of available resources. Third, structure can be perceived as the embedded relations required to provide essential services to students.

This final chapter urges the school leader to undertake a methodical approach for selecting, sequencing, and delivering effective instruction to English learners through a comprehensive model for instructional improvement. Through the examination of organizational structures from both the micro and the macro perspectives, this chapter synthesizes the salient points highlighted in the preceding chapters and brings everything together coherently for the school leader. This last chapter hones in on an array of leadership dynamics for establishing solid, sustainable school structures so that English learner reform efforts can be sustained. As such, this chapter explores how leaders can use alignment to bring together disjointed aspects in schools by navigating the reader through a comprehensive model for instructional improvement for English learners. This model offers suggestions for redesigning entire school systems and impacting the quality of instruction for English learners in the classroom. Many school leaders with English learner populations lack training on the basics of second language acquisition programming. Additionally, teachers lack the skill set they need to produce second language development in English learners. With this premise in mind, this chapter maps out a course of action for the school leader.

The model proposed in this chapter is agnostic to a given reform effort. In other words, the alignment of school structures is not contingent on a particular reform. Instead, this alignment effort is a preface for establishing reform readiness. The preceding chapters in this book should be referenced in the application and meaning-making of this model as they offer a sound research base from which to make informed decisions on improving English learner programming.

To fully leverage the instructional improvement model, a philosophical caveat merits discussion. Callahan (2005) asserts that a deficit mindset dominates the discourse on English learners in schools where language is perceived as a liability. The vernacular for discussing English learners is contingent on a shared understanding of the significance of the English language and its acquisition. The researcher argues that terms commonly used in schools such as *English Learner*, *limited English proficient*, and *sheltered English* define students with respect to linguistic deficiency. This deficit posturing of English learners enables the marginalization of linguistic minority students in U.S. schools. Prior to embarking on a course of action, this deficit thinking should be given rapt attention by a school leader. Joseph and Reigeluth (2005) argue that a fundamental rethinking of the way learning is structured for students is required for educational reform to be successful in impacting student learning. An exposé of this deficit thinking is a prerequisite to effectively utilize the instructional improvement model featured in this chapter.

UNDERSTANDING CHANGE AS A PROCESS

Understanding the process of change in schools is an apt forerunner to the application of the model. Since the model calls for a comprehensive, thoughtful approach to school reform, a leader's methodical tactic merits discussion. The critical role of leadership in the change process is established in the literature. Marks and Nance (2007) argue that to influence curricular and instructional improvement, school principals develop and nurture collaborative relationships among teachers. These leaders' efforts and influence are directed and facilitated toward continuous improvement and the attainment of a school's performance goals. This continuous improvement process constitutes organizational change in schools.

The process of change, however, is an interesting dynamic that is inarguably inevitable in schools yet rarely addressed directly. Researchers have long faulted educators' approach to change. Joseph and Reigeluth (2005) contend that the educational change literature is severely lacking in research on the process of change in education, and many educators and researchers are now calling for the development of a process knowledge base that a school community can use to sustain reform.

Drawing on evidence from various state-level reform initiatives, Fusarelli and Fusarelli (2003) highlighted the ways in which reform appears to positively impact organizational change in schools. The researchers found that reform initiatives are commonly uneven across school districts and often produce unintended consequences, including perverse incentives to lower academic standards for students to give the appearance of making adequate yearly progress toward reform objectives.

Confrey et al. (2000) maintain that to effectively manage reform, leaders typically select a unit of the school as an effort to bring about incremental change. A unit of change is a part of the whole, which is selected for its power to initiate and generate further change. Although the unit of change involves all the components of a school system, it concentrates the staging of change on a manageable set of activities. Unfortunately, comprehensiveness and the selection of a unit of change are alone insufficient for systemic improvement in schools.

Fullan (1996) warns that if reforms are to be effective, then efforts to improve schools cannot be piecemeal, but rather require comprehensiveness. The assumption is that inconsistency (lack of alignment) impedes progress. Piecemeal change only results in local change, whose sustainability is unlikely as the marginalized or ignored factors eventually overwhelm the pockets of innovation.

As opposed to incremental change, systemic reform is an approach to school change that recognizes the complexity of the school system and its interlocking parts (National Science Foundation [NSF], 1996). The piecemeal approach to change common in many schools uses a patching-up approach and focuses on a small piece of the puzzle in improving the structures of the school system that need fixing. Most school change, according to Reigeluth (1994), is inherently not systemic because it focuses on a school or a part of a school as the unit of change. True systemic change requires substantial changes in all aspects of a school.

Chapter 2 discussed a reform distortion model as a visual representation of why change efforts seem to dilute prior to infiltrating the classroom. Equally disconcerting, even when the classroom walls become permeable, there are belief-based resistance structures to contend with. No one would argue that the classroom is the ultimate unit of change in most reform efforts. Subsequently, teacher commitment is essential to any reform effort. Without teachers' commitment to improve curriculum and instruction, argue Marks and Nance (2007), principals would be hard-pressed to resolve issues in these areas affecting improved student performance.

A clear understanding of the change process is nonnegotiable for the reform-minded leader. Gándara and Rumberger's (2006) research found that school leadership is a critical factor in the success of schools serving large numbers of English learners. Principals of successful schools address the change process and have a plan of action for how English learners are to be served. This plan is articulated clearly and consistently to their staff. These leaders also redistribute resources to attend to the specific needs of English learners. Most important, these leaders press teachers for tangible academic gains for their English learners. Finally, these principals give serious attention to what professional development is needed and what materials are required to support teachers in addressing the English learner needs in the classroom.

A COMPREHENSIVE MODEL FOR ENGLISH LEARNER INSTRUCTIONAL IMPROVEMENT

Having learned of the ramifications of perceived change in schools, the school improvement process begins with a thorough analysis of the strengths and weaknesses of all dimensions of the school, resulting in the creation of a strategic direction with broad instructional goals, specific learning objectives, and detailed action plans (Beecher & Sweeny, 2008). Caution, however, should be heeded when considering the multitude of solutions available in the literature as well as commercially. Duffy, Rogerson, and Blick (2000) warn of the plethora of school improvement formulas where very few of the approaches address how to redesign entire school systems for high performance.

Researchers have long called for a more systematic approach to instructional improvement as opposed to a piecemeal tactic. Torgesen et al. (2007) advocate for the integration of all elements of a school into a comprehensive program of instruction as an approach to school improvement. The model outlined in this segment (see Figure 9.1) is designed to address what Genesee, Lindholm-Leary, Saunders, and Christian (2006) refer to as a comprehensive framework for selecting, sequencing, and delivering instruction over the course of an entire year.

The primary goal of this model is sustainable, increased academic performance of English learners through effective school reform. This model is structured around a synthesis of the work outlined in the previous chapters. It offers a series of classroom practices that school leaders can consider in addressing English learner academic needs in their schools. The model is defined by rotating concentric circles representing three prominent and intertwined dimensions. The dimension closest to the epicenter is represented by the six key factors of English learner improvement advocated by the Center for Applied Linguistics (Short & Fitzsimmons, 2007). The middle

Figure 9.1. A Comprehensive Model for Instructional Improvement for English Learners

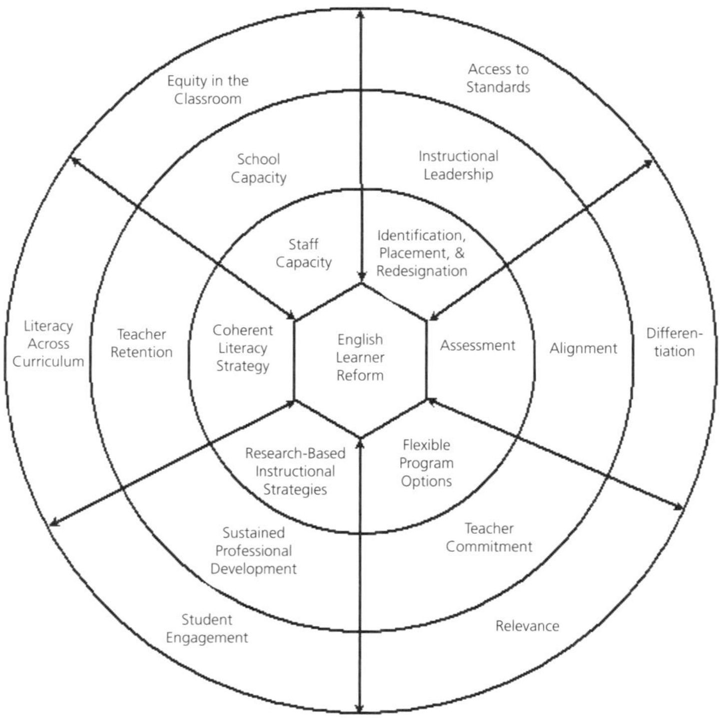

dimension represents the research-based indicators (Taylor, 2006) shown to sustain reform efforts. Combined, the components of these two dimensions make up the sustainability framework, which has been the nexus of this book. The outermost dimension represents classroom practices that aim at instructional improvement for English learners. The model advocates for six potent classroom characteristics that, when embedded in the instructional process, will increase English learner academic achievement. The use of the model is best undertaken by working outwardly clockwise, lending further credence to the model as a system of thinking—a way of school life.

To use the model for mapping a course of action, the leader is encouraged to consider two key and intertwined dimensions at a given time. This scheme is used for redesigning teaching and learning in support of English learners. The rich background of the components of the model must be activated to transform teaching and learning as part of a coherent redesign. The model is designed for making the complex pieces of English learner reform comprehensible to school leaders. Furthermore, the model is conceived in such a manner as to help educators effectively educate both majority and minority students across subject matters, curricula, cultures, and language groups, as called for by Genesee et al. (2006). The model does not endorse a specific reform or program. Instead, it establishes a road map for instruction improvement for English learners. The sections that follow address each of the key components of the model.

Access to Standards

Gándara and Rumberger (2006) articulate a blatant truth about English learner programming: that few linguistic minorities are expected or given the academic tools to achieve to the same standards as their English-speaking peers in spite of the rhetoric of school reform. These students are foreclosed from equal educational opportunity because they do not have sufficient proficiency in English to fully access the academic curriculum of schools. They are generally viewed simply in terms of where they are along the continuum toward English proficiency and this perspective serves only to impede the focus on academic performance (Olsen, 2010a). The self-defeating structural culprit behind the denying of equal access to standards to English learners resides in the flawed placement of English learners in the classroom. To remedy this, Edvantia (2007) recommends basing assessment policies and English learner redesignation decisions on measures of students' proficiency in academic English.

There is a history of inconsistent placements of English learners. As Chapter 2 demonstrated, many English learners have experienced the ping pong effect of placement in one kind of program for a period of time, then into another kind of program, and back again. Each move in and out of a program results in gaps not only in language development but also in access to academic content (Olsen, 2010b). These knowledge fragments in English learners persist and, with time, intensify, have a compounding effect, and contribute to the pervasive achievement gap common in schools.

In addition to the revolving-door policy, many schools with large numbers of English learners have largely cut out science, arts, and social studies to allow increased time for English and math in response to unsatisfactory achievement in language arts and math. This dynamic contributes to knowledge gaps and results in fewer opportunities to develop the academic language required for success in those subjects (Olsen, 2010b). There is however, an enormous downside to this dilemma. The methods currently used to classify and place English learners may result in some students' being pulled out of English language support programs too soon. To help these students get back on track, leaders should monitor the academic progress of English learners who exit language support programs and provide extra help when needed (Edvantia, 2007).

Ensuring English learners access to curriculum in the classroom requires an instructional leader with vigilance and thoughtful attention to the ramifications of English learner identification, placement, and the redesignation process. Gándara and Rumberger (2006) note that how it happens that students are reclassified as English speakers is an important policy area, and one that has resource implications as well. A number of criteria are used to determine whether linguistic minorities are English learners or fluent English-proficient and these criteria differ for students' initial classification when they first enter school and for subsequent reclassification.

Following the logic outlined by the model, equal access to standards for English learners begins with a solid identification, placement, and redesignation structure in place. Instructional leaders are encouraged to use the structure to scaffold and ensure that English learners have equal access to standards in the classroom. The placement and redesignation processes have a direct bearing on this decision. Potent conversations with teachers can be hosted using the model to articulate the topic of English learners' access to core curriculum.

Differentiation

Having addressed equal access to core curriculum for English learners, the model moves clockwise to address the importance of differentiation of instruction for English learners. Differentiation is an understated yet highly effective necessity in the English learner classroom. Beecher and Sweeny (2008) divulge that differentiation is a method to improve the learning environment based on evidence that engagement in learning is enhanced when students' interests and choices are considered, and the need to provide learning experiences that are responsive to the learning characteristics of a diverse student population.

The concept is further clarified by Tomlinson (2001), who explains that in its simplistic form, differentiating instruction requires scrutinizing what goes on in the classroom, affording students multiple options for taking in information, making sense of ideas, and expressing what they learn. Differentiating instruction provides different avenues to acquiring content, to processing or making sense of ideas, and to developing products so that each student can learn effectively. The presence of English learners in a classroom magnifies the importance of differentiated instruction. Teachers who differentiate instruction carefully consider their students' various abilities, skills, and interests, then strategically plan lessons to accommodate differences among students, thereby increasing the likelihood of success for each student (Edvantia, 2007).

For obvious reasons, the precursors to effective differentiation are valid assessments that are aligned to what is being taught in the classroom. As Chapter 4 showed, providing an adequate education for English learners requires valid diagnostic, formative, and summative assessments. Gándara and Rumberger (2006) contend that diagnostic assessments are needed to effectively evaluate the skills and abilities of English learners in both their primary language and English. Formative assessments are needed to provide teachers with ongoing information on the progress of linguistic minority students in both language development and subject-matter competence. Summative assessments are needed to measure the progress of linguistic minority students in reaching standards and other outcomes, including non-cognitive outcomes. When coordinated properly, these three types of assessments provide the classroom teacher with accurate profiles of the needs of the English learners. Moreover, accurate assessment of students' skills can accelerate students' learning, allowing teachers to build on what students already know, rather than assuming that these students know nothing. This can be especially critical in upper grades where students who have received a formal education in other settings are often placed in courses that are below their skill level, placing them further behind than they need to be.

Rock, Gregg, Ellis, and Gable (2008) convey that on the basis of aligned, valid assessments, it is possible to think about differentiating instruction in three ways: (1) teachers can consider adjusting the content, process, or product of teaching and learning; (2) teachers can vary their expectations for task completion within a single lesson or across a unit of instruction; and (3) teachers can make use of a variety of graphic organizers, reading materials at different levels of complexity, direct instruction in small groups, previewing, and scaffolding strategies. Beyond English learners, all students benefit from a variety of instructional methods and supports and an appropriate balance between the challenge of instruction and the opportunity for success.

Relevance

Adhering to the path outlined in the model, the next dimension is that of relevance for English learners. At its most fundamental level, relevance has to do with the basic learning principle that learners pay attention to information that appears relevant to them; they construct relevant representations of such information, and process these representations in a context that maximizes its relevance (Sperber & Wilson, 1995).

Advocating for increased relevance in classroom pedagogy, Olsen (2010a) articulates basic precepts for more effectively meeting the needs of English learners: Recognition of the distinct needs of English learners, the need to address both academic gaps and language development, the importance of rigor and relevance, and integration with other students must be achieved without sacrificing access.

Schlechty's (2002) seminal work on the topic of relevance in the instructional process offers potent applications for enhancing English learner instruction. The researcher defines the concept of relevance as those tasks, activities, and experiences that teachers design for students and those that teachers encourage students to design for themselves, which the teacher assumes will result in students' learning what is intended that they should learn. Relevance is an effort intended to produce learning assumed to be essential to the continuation of the culture and the optimization of the moral and intellectual development of the individual student.

Optimizing an English learner's interest in learning is essential for both content attainment and language development. Manyak (2008) examined the impact of a relevance-enhancement approach called "daily news" where English learners were provided opportunities to share current events familiar to them. The researcher found that the activity created an ideal context for the teachers to foster the students' language development, provide explicit instruction and meaningful practice in various writing skills, and produce supplemental reading texts that captured the children's interest. The relevance-inducing strategy stood out as a meaning-centered instructional activity that drew on students' diverse language resources and created space in the classroom for their unique out-of-school experiences.

Ensuring relevance for English learners requires a specific skill set in teachers that can be attained through sustained professional development. Discouragingly, however, in a survey of 5,300 teachers of English learners in California, Gándara, Maxwell-Jolly, and Driscoll (2005) found that more than half of teachers, with 26–50% of their students designated English learners, had either zero or one in-service training session devoted to the instruction of English learners over a period of 5 years.

Student Engagement

Increased English learner engagement is achieved through meaningful and relevant instruction in the classroom. Access to core standards and effective differentiation to meet English learner needs, coupled with relevant approaches to instruction, will lead to increased student interest in learning. The model now moves on to student engagement.

Students become engaged in the learning process when they understand that the content and skills they are being asked to learn are connected to their day-to-day lives. Moll and González's (1994) research concluded that students from culturally and linguistically diverse families possess a wealth of cultural knowledge and experiences that can be used to enhance their learning in meaningful ways. Classroom instruction that embeds these students' out-of-school knowledge with the official school curriculum often generates deep engagement in significant meaning-making processes (Manyak, 2008).

Schlechty (2002) asserts that engaging students in the learning process requires teachers' purposefully creating, designing, identifying, or otherwise making available to students authentically engaging activities, programs, tasks, assignments, and opportunities that result in students' learning those things required by the district-adopted curriculum.

Just like differentiation of instruction is required for English learner academic success, so too must the differentiation in teacher professional development become a reality. Supporting teachers with varied and differentiated professional development will lead to an increase in student engagement in the classroom. Even those teachers who are well trained in teaching English learners may require a kind of professional development that differs from those teachers with less background and skill in the area (Gándara & Rumberger, 2006).

Providing the know-how for enhancing student engagement should be a strong focus for teachers of English learners that will ultimately reap beneficial pay-offs. Through a sustained professional development effort, a cadre of highly skilled teachers who embrace new ideas and strategies can emerge as staff development leaders as they collectively examine ways to improve student achievement. This core of support of teachers can develop their unique gifts and talents and gain confidence as teachers of other teachers. Their passion for the success of their students can lead to the development of the school as a professional learning community (Beecher & Sweeny, 2008).

Literacy Across the Curriculum

Working through the model, the next step is literacy across the curriculum. Chapter 7 unveiled a detailed, coherent literacy strategy for English learners. When adhered to, this strategy will result in effective literacy development for English learners across all curricular areas. McKenna and Robinson (1990) define content literacy as the ability to use reading and writing for the acquisition of new content in a given discipline.

Content-area literacy is a gateway skill set that is paramount to the academic success of English learners. Unfortunately, more often than not, literacy development is perceived to be the responsibility of the language arts teachers in many schools. However, English learner literacy cannot be the sole responsibility of the language arts teacher or the English language development teacher. For English learners to be successful in schools, effective literacy strategies should be incorporated across all curricular areas, with all teachers assuming responsibility for sound literacy development in English learners. Olsen (2010b) notes that in a decade in which there has been increasingly strong and convergent research about the important role that primary language instruction plays in developing English literacy, the number of English learners receiving primary language development or instruction has dwindled to just 5%.

Key to content-area literacy is proficiency in academic English—the kind of language used in textbooks and classrooms but not necessarily in social situations. Increasing students' opportunity to learn academic English, across content areas and grade levels, and across domains (reading, writing, speaking, and listening) can benefit both English learners and native English speakers. Middle schools and secondary school teachers, in particular, need professional development and support in helping English learners improve their reading comprehension—and their proficiency in academic English—through explicit instruction in literacy strategies, vocabulary, and background knowledge (Edvantia, 2007).

As the makeup of the student population continues to evolve, schools struggle to create effective instruction for English learners. Hawkins (2004) pleads for more research on strategies that support English learner literacy development in the middle years in particular.

Equity in the Classroom

Having gone full circle around the model, the final element is equity in the classroom. This concept shares a close relationship with its sister dimension of equal access to core curriculum. The concern for equity in the classroom for English learners can be traced to its legal origins. The landmark

Supreme Court ruling *Lau v. Nichols*, based on Title VI of the Civil Rights Law, declared that merely providing students with the same facilities, textbooks, teachers, and curriculum does not create equality of treatment for students who do not understand English and are effectively foreclosed from any meaningful education (*Lau v. Nichols*, 1973). As a result of this legislation, schools throughout the nation began to create programs focused on moving students along the continuum from non-English-speaking to limited English to English proficiency. Unfortunately, decades later, English learners continue to disproportionately end up in the lowest quartiles of academic achievement (Olsen, 2010a).

This bleak scenario has motivated practitioners as well as researchers to look more closely at the interactions between students and teachers in diverse classrooms with English learners. Bondy, Ross, Gallingane, and Hambacher (2007) investigated culturally responsive classroom management strategies, suggesting that creating safe and productive environments with a diverse student population requires more than effective instructional strategies.

Weinstein, Tomlinson-Clarke, and Curran (2004, as cited in Bondy et al., 2007) noted that equity in the classroom is manifested by teachers who (1) recognize their ethnocentrism and understand the broader sociopolitical context to understand that definitions of appropriate classroom behavior are culturally defined, (2) develop knowledge of their students' cultural backgrounds, (3) use culturally appropriate classroom-management strategies, and (4) build caring classroom communities. Supporting this contention, Hastie, Martin, and Buchannan (2006) concurred that successful use of any culturally relevant pedagogy depends on teachers' concern for the sociopolitical context and their own position within a group. For equity to be achieved, teachers must recognize that students may question teachers' credibility and authority. Finally, Ladson-Billings (1995) proposed that authentic, positive social relations in a classroom are a defining characteristic of culturally relevant pedagogy in practice.

In addition to culturally responsive teaching, equity for English learners requires different types of resources rather than additional amounts. For example, to teach oral English and other aspects of English as identified in California's ELD standards, teachers need different skills and knowledge. These teachers may need different skills, abilities, sensitivities, and knowledge of students' cultural backgrounds to effectively communicate with the parents of English learners, which includes more than simply the ability to speak their language (Gándara & Rumberger, 2006).

The model has provided an opportunity to examine six crucial classroom dynamics that, when aligned properly in a school, will increase the likelihood of English learner academic success. These dynamics can only be realized when the other two core dimensions have been adequately addressed by the school leader. This model assumes a commitment from the school leader to the continuous professional development of teachers. Professional development in meeting the educational needs of English learners cannot be overstated. It is through this professional development that teachers will come to understand why and how to increase English learners' opportunity to learn academic English. The use of this model to develop a sustained professional development program for teachers will result in the provision of a comprehensive framework, as advocated by Edvantia (2007), for delivering academic instruction to promote the success of all students, including English learners.

FINAL THOUGHTS

Gándara and Rumberger (2006) assert that while the accountability movement in the past decade has brought to light the English learner dilemma, it has also had unintended consequences on linguistic minority students. Because the states' accountability system consists of standards-based tests developed for English speakers, and makes no accommodation for the fact that English learners are, by definition, deficient in English, these tests are neither valid nor reliable indicators of what these students know and can do. The questionable assessment of English learner potential is further exacerbated by the lack of rigor in English learner programming.

This book has offered school leaders a vast array of tools to bring about successful reform for English learner academic success. This assembly of work has dealt with two current, thought-provoking themes: the leadership challenges in narrowing the English learner achievement gap, and the sustainability of reform to close said gap. In the context of school reform, this book is designed to highlight the leadership challenge of meeting the academic needs of English learners and has offered a sustainability framework and a comprehensive model for instructional improvement for English learners. This book uses a sustainability framework as a venue to explore reform efforts in relation to closing the prevalent achievement gap for English learners in schools. The core chapters have provided a progressive series of tools, exercises, and rubrics that engage the school leader and staff in analyzing and developing discussions about English learner challenges in the context of sustaining school reform. By explicitly blending the two parallel threads, English learner challenges and the sustainability framework, this book offers insightful lessons about the required skill sets of school leaders as they go about the day-to-day routines of implementing school reform.

The task of closing the English learner achievement gap is by no means a simple one. Improving academic success for English learners is a multidimensional challenge that cuts across the entire spectrum of the public education system in this country. Some challenges must be addressed at the federal or state level—for example, the alignment of state assessments and content standards, and sufficient inclusion of academic English in both. Many decisions about English learner education, however, are made locally. In making these decisions, school and district leaders need to consider the number, diversity, and mobility of the English learners being served. They must also be responsive to changes in the student population (Edvantia, 2007).

The research undergirding this entire book, along with the comprehensive model for instructional improvement for English learners, suggests the following broad recommendations:

At the district level, ensuring that curriculum and instruction reflects inclusion of first language instruction can yield long-term benefits for English learners (Edvantia, 2007). Katz (1999) found that English learner programs lack academic rigor. Successful English learner programs, according to Callahan (2005), demonstrate effective integration of content-area curricula and English language acquisition strategies. Districts can support both teachers and students in this endeavor by making sure teachers are well prepared, adopting programs that provide sustained and coherent instruction across grade levels, and fostering continuous school improvement with a focus on student learning. Although literacy across content areas is critical for English learner success, replacing English language development with a reading intervention can be detrimental to English learner academic achievement (Edvantia, 2007).

At the school level, the leader's role in providing professional development that will result in an increase in English learner engagement is pivotal. The staff development program must be closely monitored and adjusted as needed. Successful professional development is characterized by teachers being given the tools and the support to be able to successfully implement the concepts presented. In examining characteristics of effective professional development for teachers of English learners, Beecher and Sweeny (2008) concluded that training, modeling, and coaching were at the forefront. Effective staff development occurs during biweekly grade-level seminars, monthly staff meetings, and weekly school or district staff development sessions. With time, teachers become curriculum developers and trainers, and content-area experts can be called upon to support the staff development efforts when necessary.

Many of the attributes of effective schools can also support English learner achievement. Factors that can contribute to the success of English learners include schoolwide commitment to English learner achievement, consistent language support services of adequate duration across all grade levels, sufficient educator capacity, and a match between resources and the community served (Edvantia, 2007).

The process of changing a school culture for English learner success is multifaceted. It involves effort by many individuals, extends over time, and requires attention to every component of the school day and curriculum. Reducing the achievement gap involves changing the teaching and learning paradigm from one of remediation to a strength-based, student-centered methodology of enrichment teaching and learning (Beecher & Sweeny, 2008).

At the classroom level, helping individual English learners master academic language is an intricate, long-term process, not an event or a program with a clear deadline. Misconceptions about how children learn languages are rampant. Teachers need to be aware of these misconceptions and realize that quick and easy solutions are not appropriate for complex problems. Second language learning by this country's public school students takes longer, is harder, and involves more effort than many teachers realize (Edvantia, 2007).

Examining the pervasive student achievement gap in public schools shows that English learners are over-represented. Large numbers of these English learners are leaving school, with and without high school diplomas, barely able to read and write or possessing even the simplest of basic skills. This book has illustrated the simple, undisputable fact that the English learner population in this country's public school system is on the rise and shows no sign of slowing down. It also has made transparent the fact that this nation's public schools are ill-prepared to meet the academic needs of this rapidly increasing student population. Although the plight of the English learner in the U.S. public school system is not without political implications, the issue of addressing their academic needs is one of a moral as well as ethical imperative. If indeed demographers are correct, and there is no reason to suspect otherwise, this population of students is predicted to become the majority within the next few decades. Does it not then make sense to have a well-educated majority? Indeed, enough is known to bridge the English learner achievement gap now.

References

Abedi, J., & Dietel, R. (2004). *Challenges in the No Child Left Behind Act for English Language Learners.* (CRESST Policy Brief No. 7). Los Angeles, CA: National Center for Research in Evaluation, Standards, and Student Testing. Retrieved from http://www.cse.ucla.edu/products/policy/cresst_policy7.pdf

Academic Information Management, Inc. (AIM). (2003). *Follow-up study of schools implementing comprehensive school reform in the Southwest.* Austin, TX: Southwest Educational Development Laboratory.

Agullard, K., Huebner, T. A., Goughnour, D., & Calisi-Corbett, G. (2005). *The impact of three different approaches to districtwide continuous improvement.* San Francisco, CA: WestEd.

Anderson, R. C., Wilson, P. T., & Fielding, L. G. (1988). Growth in reading and how children spend their time outside of school. *Reading Research Quarterly, 23*(3), 285–303.

Argyris, C. (1993). *Knowledge for action: A guide to overcoming barriers to organizational change.* San Francisco, CA: Jossey-Bass.

Artiles, A. J., & Ortiz, A. A. (Eds.). (2002). *English language learners with special education needs: Identification, assessment, and instruction.* Washington, DC, and McHenry, IL: Center for Applied Linguistics and Delta Systems.

August, D. (2002). *English as a second language instruction: Best practices to support the development of literacy for English language learners.* Baltimore, MD: Johns Hopkins University, Center for Research on the Education of Students Placed At Risk.

August, D. (2003). *Supporting the development of English literacy in English language learners: Key issues and promising practices.* Report of the Center for Research on the Education of Students Placed at Risk. Baltimore, MD: John Hopkins University.

August, D., Carlo, M., Dressler, C., & Snow, C. (2005). The critical role of vocabulary development for English language learners. *Learning Disabilities Research & Practice, 20*(1), 50–57.

August, D., & Shanahan, T. (Eds.) (2006). *Developing literacy in second-language learners: Report of the National Literacy Panel on language-minority children and youth.* Mahwah, NJ: Lawrence Erlbaum Associates.

Bailey, A. L. (2007). *The language demands of school: Putting academic English to the test.* New Haven, CT: Yale University Press.

Barnes, M., Clarke, D., & Stephens, M. (2000). Assessment: The engine of systemic curricular reform? *Journal of Curriculum Studies, 32*(5), 623–650.

Basken, P. (2006, March 29). States have more schools failing behind. *The Washington Post.* Retrieved from http://washington- post.com/wp-dyn/content/article/2006/03/28/ AR2006032801794.html

Batalova, J., Fix, M., & Murray, J. (2005). *English language learner adolescents: Demographics and literacy achievements.* Report to the Center for Applied Linguistics. Washington, DC: Migration Policy Institute.

Beecher, M., & Sweeny, S. M. (2008). Closing the achievement gap with curriculum enrichment and differentiation: One school's story. *Journal of Advanced Academics, 19,* 502–530.

Bell, B., & Gilbert, J. (1996). *Teacher development: A model from science education.* London: Routledge Falmer.

Berends, M., Kirby, S. N., Naftel, S., & McKelvey, C. (2001). *Implementation and performance in New American Schools: Three years into scale-up.* Santa Monica, CA: RAND.

Berlak, H. (2001). Academic achievement, race, and reform: A short guide to understanding assessment policy, standardized tests, and anti-racist alternatives. (Unpublished essay).

Bernhardt, E. (2005). Progress and procrastination in second language reading. *Annual Review of Applied Linguistics, 25,* 133–150.

Betts, J., Zau, A., & Rice, L. (2003). *Determinants of student achievement: New evidence from San Diego.* San Francisco, CA: Public Policy Institute of California.

Biancarosa, G., & Snow, C. E. (2004). *Reading next—A vision for action and research in middle and high school literacy: A report to Carnegie Corporation of New York* (2nd ed.). Washington, DC: Alliance for Excellent Education. Retrieved from www.carnegie.org/literacy/pdf/ReadingNext.pdf

Biancarosa, G., & Snow, C. E. (2006). *Reading next—A vision for action and research in middle and high school literacy: A report from the Carnegie Corporation of New York* (2nd ed). Washington, DC: Alliance for Excellence Education.

Bondy, E., Ross, D. D., Gallingane, C., & Hambacher, E. (2007). Creating environments of success and resilience: Culturally responsive classroom management and more. *Urban Education, 42*(4), 346–348.

Borko, H., Wolf, S. A., Simone, G., & Uchiyama, K. P. (2003). Schools in transition: Reform efforts and school capacity in Washington state. *Educational Evaluation and Policy Analysis, 25*(2), 171–201.

Brown, C. J., Stroh, H. R., Fouts, J. T., & Baker, D. B. (2005). *Learning to change: School coaching for systemic reform.* Report to the Bill and Melinda Gates Foundation. Mill Creek, WA: Fouts & Associates, L.L.C.

Calderón, M., Hertz-Lazarowitz, R., & Slavin, R. E. (1998). Effects of bilingual cooperative integrated reading and composition on students making the transition

from Spanish to English reading. *Elementary School Journal, 99*(2), 153–165.
California Department of Education. *Dataquest*. (n.d.) Retrieved, from http://data1.cde.ca.gov/dataquest/

Californians Together. (2008). *English learner state and federal accountability systems survey results*. Long Beach, CA: Californians Together.

Callahan, R. M.(2006). The intersection of accountability and language: Can reading intervention replace English language development? *Bilingual Research Journal, 30*(1), 1–21.

Callahan, R. M. (2005). Tracking and high school English learners: Limiting opportunity to learn. *American Education Research Journal, 42*(2), 305–328.

Camburn, E. M., Kimball, S. M., & Lowenhaupt, R. (2008). Going to scale with teacher leadership: Lessons learned from a districtwide literacy coach initiative. In M. M. Mangin & S. R. Stoelinga (Eds.), *Effective teacher leadership: Using research to inform and reform* (pp. 120–143). New York: Teachers College Press.

Capps, R., Fix, M., Murray, J., Ost, J., Passel, J. S., & Herwantoro, S. (2005). *The new demography of America's schools: Immigration and the No Child Left Behind Act*. Washington, DC: The Urban Institute. Retrieved from http://www.urban.org/UploadedPDF/311230_new_demography.pdf

Carroll, J., & Fulton, D. (2004). The true cost of teacher turnover. *Threshold*. Retrieved from www.ciconline.org

Case, R. E. (2002). The intersection of language, education, and content: Science instruction for ESL students. *The Clearing House, 76*(2), 71–74.

Center for Public Education. (2007). *Research review: What research says about preparing English language learners for academic success*. Alexandria, VA: Author.

Center on Education Policy. (2009a). *Are achievement gaps closing and is the achievement rising for all?* Washington, DC: Author.

Center on Education Policy. (2009b). *State test score trends through 2007–08, Part 2. Is there a plateau effect in test scores?* Washington, DC: Author.

Century, J. R., & Levy, A. J. (2002). *Researching the sustainability of reform: Factors that contribute to or inhibit program endurance*. Newton, MA: Education Development Center, Inc.

Century, J. R., & Levy, A. J. (2004). *Institutionalization and sustainability: Think tank bringing theory of and research on sustainability to practice: Giving school improvement a "bottom line."* Newton, MA: Research and Evaluation Reports and Center for Science Education.

Cervetti, G. N., Bravo, M. A., Duong, T., Hernandez, S., & Tilson, J. (2008). *A research-based approach to instruction for English language learners in science*. A report to the Noyce Foundation. Berkeley, CA: University of California, Berkeley.

Choi, P. L., & Tang, S. Y. F. (2009). Teacher commitment trends: Cases of Hong Kong teacher from 1997 to 2007. *Teaching and Teacher Education, 25*, 767–777.

Chrispeels, J. H., Burke, P. H., Johnson, P., & Daly, A. J. (2008). Aligning mental models of district and school leadership teams for reform coherence. *Education and Urban Society, 40*(6), 730–750.

Christensen, C., Aaron, S., & Clark, W. (2005). Can schools improve? *Phi Delta Kappan, 86*(7), 545–550.

Coggins, C., Zuckerman, S., & McKelvey, L. A. (2011). Holding on to Gen Y. *Educational Leadership, 67*(8), 70-74.

Cohen, D. K., & Ball, D. L. (1996). *Capacity and building capacity for instruction.* Paper presented at the annual meeting of the American Education Research Association. New York, NY.

Collier, V. P. (1987). Age and rate of acquisition of language for academic purposes. *TESOL Quarterly, 21*(4), 677–741.

Collier, V. P., & Thomas, W. P. (1989). How quickly can immigrants become proficient in school English? *Journal of Educational Issues of Language Minority Students, 5*, 26–38.

Confrey, J., Castro-Filho, J., & Wilhelm, J. (2000). Implementation research as a means to link systemic reform and applied psychology in mathematics education. *Educational Psychologist, 35*(3), 179–191.

Conley, D. T. (2003). *Who governs our schools?* New York: Teachers College Press.

Conzemius, A., & O'Neill, J. (2001). *Building shared responsibility for student learning.* Alexandria: VA: Association for Supervision and Curriculum Development.

Copland, M. A. (2003). Leadership of inquiry: Building and sustaining capacity for school improvement. *Educational Evaluation and Policy Analysis, 25*(4), 375–395.

Corcoran, T., & Goertz, M. (1995). Instructional capacity and high performance schools. *Educational Researcher, 24*, 27–31.

Corcoran, T., & Lawrence, N. (2003). *Changing district culture and capacity: The impact of the Merck Institute for Science Education Partnership.* Consortium for Policy Research in Education. Philadelphia: University of Pennsylvania.

Council of Great City Schools, The (2009). *Succeeding with English Language Learners: Lessons learned from the Great City Schools.* Washington, DC: Council of the Great City Schools.

Covey, D. D. (1973). *An analytical study of secondary freshmen bilingual education and its effects on academic achievement and attitudes of Mexican American students.* Doctoral dissertation, Arizona State University.

Crowson, R. L. (2003). The turbulent policy environment in education: Implications for school administration and accountability. *Peabody Journal of Education, 78*(4), 29–43.

Crowson, R. L., & Boyd, W. (1992). Urban schools as organizations: Political perspectives. In J. Cibulka, R. Reed, & K. Wong (Eds.), *The politics of urban education in the United States* (pp. 87–105). London, England: Falmer Press.

Cuban, L. (1986). *How teachers taught: Constancy and change in American classrooms, 1890–1980.* New York: Longman.

Cummins, J. (1984). *Bilingualism and special education: Issues in assessment and pedagogy.* Clevedon, England: Multilingual Matters.

Cunningham, A. E., & Stanovich, K. E. (1997). Early reading acquisition and its relation to reading experience and ability 10 years later. *Developmental Psychology, 33*, 934–945.

Czerniak, C. M., Beltyukova, S., Struble, J., Haney, J. J., & Lumpe, A. T. (2005). Do you see what I see? The relationship between a professional development model and student achievement. In R. E. Yager (Ed.), *Exemplary science in grades 5–8: Standards-based success stories* (pp. 13–43). Arlington, VA: NSTA Press.

D'Anna, C. A., Zechmeister, E. V., & Hall, J. W. (1991). Toward a meaningful definition of vocabulary size. *Journal of Reading Behavior, 23*(1), 109–122.

Datnow, A. (2000). Power and politics in the adoption of school reform models. *Educational Evaluation and Policy Analysis, 22*(4), 357–374.

Datnow, A. (2005). The sustainability of comprehensive school reform models in changing district and state contexts. *Educational Administration Quarterly, 41*(1), 121–153.

Day, C., & Gu, Q. (2007). Variations in the conditions for teachers' professional learning and development: Sustaining commitment and effectiveness over a career. *Oxford Review of Education, 33*(4), 423–443.

Dreeben, R. (2002). *On what is learned in school.* Clinton Corners, NY: Percheron Press, Eliot Werner Inc.

Duffy, F. M., Rogerson, L. G., & Blick, C. (2000). *Redesigning America's schools: a systems approach to improvement.* Norwood, MA: Christopher-Gordon Publishers.

DuFour, R., DuFour, R., Eaker, R. & Many, T. (2006). *Learning by doing: A handbook for professional learning communities at work*. Bloomington, IN: Solution Tree.

Echevarria, J., & Graves, A. (2003). *Sheltered content instruction: Teaching English language learners with diverse abilities*. Boston, MA: Allyn & Bacon.

Echevarria, J., Short, D., & Powers, K. (2006). School reform and standards-based education. How do teachers help English language learners? *Journal of Educational Research, 95*, 1–28.

Echevarria, J., Vogt, M. E., & Short, D. (2004). *Making content comprehensible for English learners: The SIOP model*. Boston, MA: Allyn & Bacon.

Edvantia. (2007). *Research review: What research says about preparing English language learners for academic success.* Alexandria, VA: Center for Public Education.

Elmore, R. F. (1993). The role of school districts in instructional improvement. In S. H. Fuhrman (Ed.), *Designing coherent education systems* (pp. 96–124). San Francisco, CA: Jossey-Bass.

Elmore, R. F. (2000). *Building a new structure for school leadership*. Washington, DC: The Albert Shanker Institute.

Elmore, R. F. (2005). *School reform from the inside out: Policy, practice, and performance*. Cambridge, MA: Harvard Education Press.

Elmore, R. F., & Burney, D. (1997). *Improving instruction through professional development in New York City's community district #2*. [Policy Bulletin.] Consortium for Policy Research in Education. Philadelphia: University of Pennsylvania.

Elmore, R. F. & City, E. A. (2007). The road to school improvement: It's hard, it's bumpy, and it takes as long as it takes. *Harvard Education Letter, 23*(3), 1–3.

Ernst-Slavit, G., & Wenger, K. J. (2006). Teaching in the margins: The multifaceted work and struggles of bilingual paraeducators. *Anthropology & Education Quarterly, 37,* 62–82.

Evans, W., Baugh, C., Sheffer, J., Martin, G., & Scarentino, R. (2004, February). *Sustained effects of CSR programs and the relationship to No Child Left Behind requirements.* Paper presented at the annual meeting of the International Reading Association, Reno, NV.

Faltis, C. J., & Wolfe, P. M. (1999). *So much to say: Adolescents, bilingualism, and ESL in the secondary school.* New York: Teachers College Press.

Firestone, W. (1989). Using reform: Conceptualizing district initiative. *Education and Policy Analysis, 11*(2), 151–164.

Fishman, B. J., Marx, R. M., Best, S., & Tal, R. T. (2003). Linking teacher and student learning to improve professional development in systemic reform. *Teaching and Teacher Education, 19*, 643–658.

Flett, J. D., & Wallace, J. (2005). Change dilemmas for curriculum leaders: Dealing with mandated change in schools. *Journal of Curriculum and Supervision, 20*(3), 188–213.

Foorman, B. & Carlson, C. D. (2006). Is a separate block of time for oral English language development in programs for English learners needed? *The Elementary School Journal, 107*(2), 181–198.

Francis, D. J., Rivera, M., Lesaux, N., Kieffer, M., & Rivera, H. (2006). *Practical guidelines for the education of English Language Learners: Research-based recommendations for instruction and academic interventions.* Portsmouth, NH: Center on Instruction.

Freeman, Y. S., Freeman, D. E., & Mercuri, S. (2002). *Closing the achievement gap: How to reach limited-formal-schooling and long-term English learners*. Portsmouth, NH: Heinemann.

Fry, R. (2008). *The role of schools in the English language learner achievement gap*. Washington, DC: The Pew Hispanic Center.

Fuhrman, S., Clune, W. H., & Elmore, R. F. (1988). Research on education reform: Lessons on the implementation of policy. *Teachers College Record, 90*(2), 237–257.

Fullan, M. G. (2005). *Leadership and sustainability: System thinkers in action.* Thousand Oaks, CA: Corwin Press.

Fullan, M. G. (1996). Turning systemic thinking on its head. *Phi Delta Kappan, 77,* 420–423.

Fullan, M. G., Bertani, A., & Quinn, J. (2004). New lessons for districtwide reform. *Educational Leadership, 61*(7), 42–46.

Fusarelli, B. C., & Fusarelli, L. D. (2003). Systemic reform and organizational change. *Planning and Changing, 34*(3&4), 169–177.

Gándara, P., Maxwell-Jolly, J., & Driscoll, A. (2005). *Listening to teachers of English learners*. Santa Cruz, CA: Center for the Future of Teaching and Learning.

Gándara, P., & Rumberger, R. W. (2006). *Resource needs for California's English learners*. Stanford, CA: Linguistic Minority Research Institute, University of California.

Gándara, P., Rumberger, R., Maxwell-Jolly, J., & Callahan, R. (2003). English Learners in California schools: Unequal resources, unequal outcomes. *Education Policy Analysis Archives, 11*(36), 1–54.

Garcia, G. E., & Godina, H. (2004). Addressing the literacy needs of adolescent English language learners. In T. Jetton and J. Dole (Eds.), *Adolescent literacy: Research and practice* (pp. 304–320). New York: The Guildford Press.

Garcia, O., Kleifgen, J. A., & Falchi, L. (2008). *From English language learners to emergent bilinguals, equity matters: Research Review No. 1*. New York: Teachers College.

Garcia, R. (2005). Sustainability crisis: A time for resolution. *Educational Leadership & Administration, 17*, 33–46.

Garcia, R. (2009). *Benchmarking exponential growth of educational reform: The sustainability index. Educational Leadership & Administration, 21*, 72–86.

Garcia, R., Cesario, L., Stanga, K., & Mangewala, R. (2010). Systemic alignment: A precursor to sustaining English Learner academic performance. *School Leadership Review, 6*, 69–94.

Genesee, F., Lindholm-Leary, K., Saunders, W. M., & Christian, D. (2006). *Educating English language learners: A synthesis of research evidence*. New York: Cambridge University Press.

Gersten, R., & Baker, S. (2000). The professional knowledge base on instructional practices that support cognitive growth for English language learners. In R. Gersten, E. Schiller, & S. Vaughn (Eds.), *Contemporary special education research: Syntheses of the knowledge base on critical instructional issues* (pp. 31–79). Mahwah, NJ: Erlbaum.

Gersten, R., Taylor, R., & Graves, A. (1999). Direct instruction and diversity. In R. Stevens (Ed.), *Teaching in America: Teaching in American schools* (pp. 81–102). Columbus, OH: Merrill/Prentice Hall.

Goertz, M. E., Floden, R. E., & O'Day, J. (1995). *Studies of education reform: Systemic reform*. New Brunswick, NJ: Consortium for Policy Research in Education, Rutgers University.

Gomez, L., Freeman, D., & Freeman, Y. (2005). Dual language education: A promising 50-50 model. *Bilingual Research Journal, 29*(1), 145–164.

Goodman, R. M., & Steckler, A. B. (1989). A framework for assign program institutionalization. *Knowledge in Society: The International Journal of Knowledge Transfer*, 2, 57–71.

Goodson, I. F. (2001). Social histories of educational change. *Journal of Educational Change, 2*(1), 45–63.

Grant, R. A., & Wong, S. D. (2003). Barriers to literacy for language-minority learners: An argument for change in the literacy education profession. *Journal of Adolescent & Adult Literacy, 46*(5), 386–394.

Graves, A. W. (1987). Improving comprehension skills. *Teaching Exceptional Children, 19*(2), 58–67.

Graves, M. F. (2006). The *vocabulary book: Learning and instruction*. New York: Teachers College, Columbia University.

Graves, M. F., & Watts-Taffe, S. M. (2002). *The place of word consciousness in a research-based vocabulary program: What research has to say about reading instruction*. Newark, DE: International Reading Association.

Green, L. C. (2004). *Bilingual word power—research based vocabulary strategies for English language learners*. San Antonio, TX: Intercultural Development Research Association Newsletter.

Grissom, J. B. (2004). Reclassification of English Learners. *Education Policy Analysis Archives, 12*(36), 1–38. Retrieved from http://epaa.asu.edu/epaa/v12n36/

Gu, Q., & Day, C. (2006). Teachers' resilience: a necessary condition for effectiveness. *Teaching and Teacher Education, 23*, 1302–1316.

Haertel, E. H. (1999) Performance assessment and education reform. *Phi Delta Kappan, 80*(9), 662–666.

Hakuta, K., Butler, Y. G., & Witt, D. (1999). *How long does it take English language learners to attain proficiency?* Unpublished paper, Stanford, CA: Stanford University.

Hallinan, M. T. (2004). Whatever happened to the "detracking" movement? *Education Next, 4*(4), 72–76.

Hallinan, M. T., & Kubitschek, W. N. (1999). Curriculum differentiation and high school achievement. *Social Psychology of Education, 3*, 41–62.

Hallinger, P. (2003). Leading educational change: Reflections on the practice of instructional leadership and transformational leadership. *Cambridge Journal of Education, 33*(3), 329–351.

Hamann, E. T., & Reeves, J. (2008). *Accessing high-quality instructional strategies*. Davis: University of California–Davis, School of Education, Center for Applied Policy in Education.

Hansche, L. N. (1998). *Meeting the requirements of Title I: Handbook for the development of performance standards*. Washington, DC: U.S. Department of Education.

Hargreaves, A., & Fink, D. (2000). The three dimensions of reform. *Educational Leadership, 57*(7), 30–34.

Hargreaves, A., & Fink, D. (2006). *Sustainable leadership*. San Francisco, CA: Jossey-Bass.

Harklau, L. (1994). Jumping tracks: How language-minority students negotiate evaluations of ability. *Anthropology and Education Quarterly, 25*(3), 347–363.

Harris, A., & Chrispeels, J. H. (Eds.). (2006). *Improving schools and educational systems: International perspectives*. London: Routledge.

Hart, B., & Risley, T. R. (2003). The early catastrophe: The 30 million word gap. *American Educator, 27*(1), 4–9.

Hastie, P. A., Martin, E., & Buchannan, A. M. (2006). Stepping out of the norm: An examination of praxis for a culturally-relevant pedagogy for African-American children. *Journal of Curriculum Studies, 38*(3), 293–306.

Hatch, T. (1998). The differences in theory that matter in the practice of school improvement. *American Educational Research Journal, 35*(1), 3–32.

Hawkins, M. R. (2004). Researching English language and literacy development in schools. *Educational Researcher, 33*(3), 14–25. doi: 10.3102/0013189X033003014

Hayes, K., & Salazar, J. J. (2001). *Evaluation of the structured English immersion program. Final Report: Year 1*. Los Angeles, CA: Los Angeles Unified School District.

Hess, F. (1999). *Spinning wheels: The politics of urban school reform*. Washington, DC: Brookings Institution.

Hopkins, D., & Reynolds, D. (2001). The past, the present and future of school improvement: Towards the third age. *British Educational Research Journal, 27*(4), 459–475.

Hoshchild, J. (2003). Rethinking accountability politics. In P. E. Peterson & M. R. West (Eds.), *No child left behind?* (pp. 107–123). Washington, DC: Brookings Institution.

Jencks, C., & Phillips, M. (Eds.). (1998). *The Black-White test score gap*. Washington, DC: Brookings Institution.

Jepsen, C., & de Alth, S. (2005). *English learners in California schools*. San Francisco, CA: Public Policy Institute of California.

Johnson, C. C. (2007). Effective science teaching, professional development and No Child Left Behind: Barriers, dilemmas, and reality. *Journal of Science Teacher Education, 18*, 133–136.

Johnson, C. C., & Fargo, J. D. (2010). Urban school reform enabled by transformative professional development: Impact on teacher change and student learning of science. *Urban Education, 45*(1), 4–29.

Johnson, K., Hays, C., Center, H., & Daley, C. (2004). Building capacity and sustainable prevention innovations: a sustainability planning model. *Evaluation and Program Planning, 27*, 135–139.

Joseph, R., & Reigeluth, C. M. (2005). Formative research on an early stage of the systemic change process in a small school district. *British Journal of Educational Technology, 36*(6), 937–956.

Katz, S. R. (1999). Teaching in tensions: Latino immigrant youth, their teachers and the structures of schooling. *Teachers College Record, 100*, 809–840.

Kaufman, M. (1968). Will instruction in reading Spanish affect ability in reading English? *Journal of Reading, 11*, 521–527.

Keefe, J. W., & Amenta, R. B. (2005). What ever happened to the model schools project? *Phi Delta Kappan, 86*(7), 536–544.

Kelly, S. (2007). The contours of tracking in North Carolina. *The High School Journal, 90*(4), 15–31.

Knapp, M. S., Copland, M. A., Ford, B., Markholt, A., McLaughlin, M. W., Milliken, M., & Talbert, J. E. (2003). *Leading for learning sourcebook: Concepts and examples*. Center for the Study of Teaching and Policy. Seattle, WA: University of Washington. Retrieved from http://depts.washington.edu/ctpmail/PDFs/LforLSourcebook-02-03.pdf

Knight, S. L., & Erlandson, D. A. (2003). Harnessing complexity: A framework for analyzing school reform. *Planning and Changing, 34*(3-4), 178–196.

Kruse, S. D. (2008). Reflections on leading and learning for change. *Education and Urban Society, 40*(6), 655–669.

La Marca, P. M., Redfield, D., & Winter, P. C. (2000). *State standards and the state assessment systems: A guide to alignment*. Washington, D.C.: Council of Chief State School Officers.

Labaree, D. F. (2007, September). *Limits on the impact of educational reform: The case of progressivism and U.S. schools, 1900–1950*. Paper presented at the conference on "The Century of the School: Continuity and Innovation During the First Half of the 20th Century, Ascona, Switzerland.

Ladson-Billings, G. (1995). Toward a theory of culturally relevant pedagogy. *American Educational Research Journal, 32*(3), 465–491.

Ladson-Billings, G. (2006). 2006 Presidential Address: From the achievement gap to the education debt: Understanding achievement in U.S. schools. *Educational Researcher 35*(7), 3–12.

Lara, J. (2001). *Summary of state responses to informal survey: Assessing limited English proficient (LEP) students*. Washington, DC: Council of Chief State School Officers.

Lau v. Nichols. 48FF.2d791, United States Court of Appeals, Ninth Circuit, January 1973.

Leithwood, K., Jantzi, D., & Steinbach, R. (1999). *Changing leadership for changing times*. Buckingham, UK: Open University Press.

Lesaux, N. K., Kieffer, M. J., Faller, S. E., & Kelley, J. G. (2010). The effectiveness and ease of implementation of an academic vocabulary intervention for linguistically diverse students in urban middle schools. *Reading Research Quarterly, 45*(2), 196–228.

Lewis, L., Parsad, B., Carey, N., Bartfai, N., Farris, E., Smerdon, B., & Green. B. (1999). *Teacher quality: A report on the preparation of public school teachers*. (NCES 1999-080). Washington, DC: National Center for Education Statistics. Retrieved from http://nces.ed.gov/pubs99/1999080.pdf

Lindholm-Leary, K. & Genesee, F. (2010). Alternative educational programs for English language learners. In California Department of Education (Eds.),

Research on English language learners. Sacramento, CA: California Department of Education Press.

Linquanti, R. (2001). *The redesignation dilemma: Challenges and choices in fostering meaningful accountability for English learners* (Report No. 2001-1). Oakland: University of California Linguistic Minority Research Institute.

Little, J. W. (1999, April). *Teachers' professional development in the context of high school reform: Findings from a three-year study of restructuring schools*. Paper presented at the annual meeting of the American Educational Research Association, Montreal Quebec, Canada.

Little, J. W. (2001). Teachers' work at the turn of the century. In J. Oelkers (Ed.), *Futures of education: Essays from an interdisciplinary symposium* (pp. 281–303). Bern, Switzerland: Peter Lang.

Little, J. W., & Bartlett, L. (2002). Career and commitment in the context of comprehensive school reform. *Teachers and Teaching: Theory and Practice, 8*(3/4), 345–354.

Long, V. M., & Benson, C. (1998). Re-Alignment. *The Mathematics Teacher, 91*(6), 503–508.

Lortie, D. C. (1975). *Schoolteacher: A sociological study*. Chicago, IL: University of Chicago Press.

Loucks-Horsley, S., Love, N., Stiles, K. E., Mundry, S., & Hewson, P. W. (2003). *Designing professional development for teachers of mathematics and science.* Thousand Oaks, CA: Corwin Press.

MacSwan, J., & Pray, L. (2005). Learning English bilingually: Age of onset of exposure and rate of acquisition among English language learners in a bilingual education program. *Bilingual Research Journal, 29*(3), 653–678. Retrieved from http://brj.asu.edu/content/vol29_no3/art9.pdf

Mahon, E. A. (2006). High-stakes testing and English language learners: Questions of validity. *Bilingual Research Journal, 30*(2), 479–497. Retrieved from http://brj.asu.edu/vol30_no2/art11.pdf

Malen, B., & Rice, J. K. (2004). A framework for assessing the impact of education reform on school capacity: Insights from studies of high-stakes accountability initiatives. *Educational Policy, 18*(5), 631–660.

Mangin, M. M. (2009). Literacy coach role implementation: How district context influences reform efforts. *Educational Administration Quarterly, 45*(5), 759–792.

Manyak, P. C. (2008). What's your news? Portraits of a rich language and literacy activity for English- language learners. *The Reading Teacher, 61*(6), 450–458.

Marks, H. M., & Louis, K. S. (1997). Does teacher empowerment affect the classroom? The implications of teacher empowerment for teachers' instructional practice and student academic performance. *Educational Evaluation and Policy Analysis, 19*(3), 245–275.

Marks, H. M., & Nance, J. P. (2007). Contexts of accountability under systemic reform: Implications for principal influence on instruction and supervision. *Educational Administration Quarterly, 43*(1), 3–37.

Marzano, R. J. (2004). *Building background knowledge for academic achievement.* Alexandria, VA: Association of Supervision and Curriculum Development.

Massell, D. (1998). *State strategies for building capacity in education: Progress and continuing challenges.* Report of the Consortium for Policy Research in Education. Philadelphia: University of Pennsylvania.

MassPartners for Public Schools. (2005). *Facing reality: What happens when good schools are labeled "failures?" Projecting adequate yearly progress in Massachusetts schools.* Retrieved from www.massteacher.org/news/headlines/aypreport.pdf

Matsumura, L. C., Sartoris, M., Bickel, D. D., & Garnier, H. E. (2009). Leadership for literacy coaching: The principal's role in launching a new coaching program. *Educational Administration Quarterly, 45*(5), 655–693.

Maxwell-Jolly, J., Gándara, P., & Mendes-Benavidez, L. (2007). *Promoting academic literacy among secondary English language learners: A synthesis of research and practice.* Davis, CA: University of California Linguistic Minority Research Institute, Education Policy Center.

McKenna, M. C., & Robinson, R. D. (1990). Content literacy: A definition and implications. *Journal of Reading, 34,* 184–186.

McKeown, M. G., & Beck, I. L. (2005). *Direct and rich vocabulary instruction: Vocabulary instruction: Research to practice.* New York: Guilford Publications.

Meltzer, J., & Hamann, E. T. (2006). Literacy for English Learners and regular students, too. *Principal Leadership,* 6, 32–40.

Menken, K., & Kleyn, T. (2010). The long-term impact of subtractive schooling in the educational experiences of secondary English Language Learners. *International Journal of Bilingual Education and Bilingualism.* London, UK: Routledge.

Mickelson, R. (2001). Subverting Swann: First- and second-generation segregation in Charlotte- Mecklenburg schools. *American Educational Research Journal, 38*(2), 215–252.

Mintrop, H. (2004). *Schools on probation.* New York: Teachers College.

Miramontes, O. B. (1987). Oral reading miscues of Hispanic students: Implications for assessment of learning disabilities. *Journal of Learning Disabilities, 20,* 627–632.

Mitchell, D. E., Destino, T., Karam, R. T., & Colon-Muniz, A. (1999). The politics of bilingual education. *Educational Policy, 13*(1), 86–103.

Moje, E. B., Ciechanowski, K. M., Kramer, K., Ellis, L., Carrillo, R., & Collazo, T. (2004).Working toward third space in content area literacy: An examination of everyday funds of knowledge and discourse. *Reading Research Quarterly, 39*(1), 38–69.

Moll, L., & González, N. (1994). Lessons from research with language-minority children. *Journal of Reading Behavior, 26,* 439–456.

Nagy, W. E., García, G. E., Dyrgunoglu, A., & Hancin, B. (1993). Spanish-English bilingual children's use and recognition of cognates in English reading. *Journal of Reading Behavior, 25*(3), 241–259.

National Clearinghouse for English Language Acquisition and Language Instruction Educational Programs (NCELA). (2007). *FAQ: Which tests are commonly used to determine English language proficiency?* Retrieved from http://www.ncela.gwu.edu/expert/faq/25tests.htm

National Reading Panel. (2000). *Report of the national reading panel: Teaching children to read.* Washington, DC: National Institute of Child Health and Human Development.

National Science Foundation (NSF). (1996). *REC indicator series: The learning curve: What are we discovering about U.S. science and mathematics education?* (NSF Report No. 96-53). Washington, DC: Author.

Nichols, S. N., Glass, G. V., & Berliner, D. C. (2006). High-stakes testing and student achievement: Does accountability pressure increase student learning? *Education Policy Analysis Archives, 14*(1). Retrieved from http://epaa.asu.edu/epaa/v14n1/v14n1.pdf

No Child Left Behind Act of 2001, Pub. L. No. 107-110, 115 Stat. 1425 (2002).

Noell, G. H., & Gansle, K. A. (2009). Moving from good ideas in educational systems change to sustainable program implementation: Coming to terms with some of the realities. *Psychology in the Schools, 46*(1), 78–88.

Noguera, P. (2004). Transforming high schools. *Educational Leadership, 61*(8), 26–31.

Nunnery, J., Slavin, R., Ross, S., Smith, L., Hunter, P., & Stubbs, J. (1997, March). *Effects of full and partial implementations of Success for All on student reading achievement in English and Spanish.* Paper presented at the annual meeting of the American Educational Research Association, Chicago, IL.

Oakeley, C., & Urrabazo, T. (2001, April). *New state LEP testing policy in Texas: Is it an appropriate accountability measure for recent ESL immigrants?* Paper presented at the annual meeting of the American Educational Research Association, Seattle, WA. (ERIC No. ED454705)

Oakes, J. (1985). *Keeping track: How schools structure inequality.* New Haven, CT: Yale University Press.

Olsen, L. (2010a). Changing course for long term English learners. *Leadership,* November/December [special issue].

Olsen, L. (2010b). *Reparable harm: Fulfilling the unkept promise of educational opportunity for long term English learners.* Long Beach, CA: California Together.

Palmer, D. (2007). A dual immersion strand programme in California: Carrying out the promise of dual language education in an English-dominant context. *The International Journal of Bilingual Education and Bilingualism, 10*(6), 752–768.

Park, V., & Datnow, A. (2008). Collaborative assistance in a highly prescribed school reform model: The case for Success for All. *Peabody Journal of Education, 83,* 400–422.

Parrish, T. B., Perez, M., Merickel, A., & Linquanti, R. (2006). *Effects of the implementation of Proposition 227 on the education of English learners, K–12: Findings from a five-year evaluation.* Washington, DC: American

Institutes for Research and WestEd. Retrieved from http://www.air.org/news/documents/227Report.pdf

Pemberton, J. B., Rademacher, J. A., Tyler-Wood, T., and Perez-Cereijo, M. V. (2006). Aligning assessments with state curriculum standards and teaching strategies. *Intervention in School and Clinic, 41*(5), 283–289.

Penuel, W., Fishman, B. J., Gallagher, L. P., Korbak, C., & Lopez-Prado, B. (2009). Is alignment enough? Investigating the effects of state policies and professional development on science curriculum implementation. *Science Education 93*, 656–677.

Peregoy, S. F., & Boyle, O. F. (2008). *Reading, writing, and learning in ESL: A resource book for teaching K–12 English learners* (5th ed.). Boston, MA: Pearson Education.

Planty, M., Hussar, W., Snyder, T., Provasnik, S., Kena, G., Dinkes, R., KewalRamani, A., & Kemp, J. (2008). The condition of education 2008 (NCES 2008-031). Washington, DC: National Center for Education Statistics, Institute of Education Sciences, U.S. Department of Education.

Proposition 227 on the education of English learners, K–12: Year 3 report. California Department of Education, Sacramento, CA.

Purcell-Gates, V., Duke, N. K., & Martineau, J. A. (2007). Learning to read and write genre-specific text: Roles of authentic experience and explicit teaching. *Reading Research Quarterly, 42*(1), 8–45.

Rabinowitz, S., & Sato, E. (2006, April). *Technical adequacy of assessments for alternate student populations: Technical review of high-stakes assessment for English language learners*. Paper presented at the annual meeting of the National Council on Measurement in Education, San Francisco, CA.

Reese, L., Garnier, H., Gallimore, R., & Goldenberg, C. (2000). Longitudinal analysis of the antecedents of emergent Spanish literacy and middle-school English reading achievement of Spanish speaking students. *American Educational Research Journal, 37*(3), 633–662.

Reigeluth, C. M. (1994). The imperative for systemic change. In C. M. Reigeluth & R. J. Garfinkle (Eds.), *Systemic change in education* (pp. 3–11). Englewood Cliffs, NJ: Educational Technology Publications.

Reitzug, U. C., West, D. L., & Angel, R. (2008). Conceptualizing instructional leadership. *Education and Urban Society, 40*(6), 694–714.

Renzulli, L. A., Parrott, H. M., & Beattie, I. R. (2011). Racial mismatch and school type: Teacher satisfaction and retention in charter and traditional public schools. *Sociology of Education, 84*(1), 23–48.

Richard-Amato, P. A., & Snow, M. A. (2005). *Academic success for English language learners*. White Plain, NY: Pearson Education, Inc.

Rivet, A. E., & Krajcik, J. S. (2004). Achieving standards in urban systemic reform: An example of a sixth grade project-based science curriculum. *Journal of Research in Science Teaching, 41*, 669–692.

Rock, M. L., Gregg, M., Ellis, E., & Gable, R. A. (2008). REACH: A framework for differentiating classroom instruction. *Preventing School Failure, 52*(2), 31-47.

Rodríguez, T. A. (2001). From the known to the unknown: Using cognates to teach English and Spanish-speaking literates. *The Reading Teacher, 54*(8), 744–746.

Rowan, B., Correnti, R., Miller, R. J., & Camburn, E. M. (2009). School improvement by design: Lessons from a study of comprehensive school reform programs. *Consortium for Policy Research in Education* (CPRE Research Paper). Philadelphia, PA.

Rumberger, R. W. (2006). The growth of the linguistic minority population in the U.S. and California, 1980–2005. *University of California Linguistic Minority Research Institute, 8*, 1–2.

Rumberger, R. W., & Tran, L. (2006). *Preschool participation and the cognitive and social development of language minority students* (CSE Technical Report 674). Los Angeles, CA: National Center for Research on Evaluation, Standards, and Student Testing [UCLA]. Retrieved from http://lmri.ucsb.edu/publications/06_rumberger-tran.pdf

Samson, J. F., & Collins, B.A. (2012). *Preparing all teachers to meet the needs of English language learners: Applying research to policy and practice for teacher effectiveness.* Washington, DC: Center for American Progress.

Santa Clara Unified School District. (nd). *English Learner Master Plan*. Santa Clara, CA: Author

Saunders, W. M., & Goldenberg, C. (1999). *The effects of a comprehensive language arts transition program on the literacy development of English language learners.* Santa Cruz, CA: Center for Research on Education, Diversity, and Excellence, University of California.

Scarcella, R. (1996). Secondary education in California and second language research: Instructing ESL students in the 1990s. *CATESO Journal, 9*, 129–152.

Scarcella, R. (2003). *Academic English: A conceptual framework*. Los Angeles: University of California Language Minority Research Institute.

Schlechty, P. C. (2002). *Working on the work: An action plan for teachers, principals, and superintendents*. San Francisco, CA: Jossey-Bass.

Schmoker, M. (2006). *Results now: How we can achieve unprecedented improvements in teaching and learning*. Alexandria, VA: Association for Supervision and Curriculum Development.

Shannon, G. S., & Bylsma, P. (2004). *Characteristics of improved school districts: Themes from research*. Olympia, WA: Office of Superintendent of Public Instruction.

Short, D., & Fitzsimmons, S. (2007). *Double the work: Challenges and solutions to acquiring language and academic literacy for adolescent English language learners.* (A report to Carnegie Corporation of New York.) Washington, DC: Alliance for Excellent Education. Retrieved from http://www.carnegie.org/literacy/pdf/DoubletheWork.pdf

Sipple, J. W., & Killeen, K. M. (2004). Context, capacity, and concern: A district-level analysis of the implementation of standards-based reform in New York state. *Educational Policy, 18*(3), 456–490.

Slater, L. (2008). Pathway to building leadership capacity. *Educational Management, Administration & Leadership, 10,* 55–69.

Slavin, R. E., & Cheung, A. (2003). *Effective reading programs for English language learners: A best- evidence synthesis: Report of the Center for Research on the education of students placed at risk.* Baltimore, MD: John Hopkins University.

Snipes, J., Doolittle, F., & Herlihy, C. (2002). *Foundations for success: Case studies of how urban school systems improve student achievement.* Washington DC: MDRC for the Council of the Great City Schools.

Snow, C. E., Burns, M. S., & Griffin, P. (Eds.). (1998). *Preventing reading difficulties in young children.* Washington, DC: National Academy Press.

Solano-Flores, G., & Trumbull, E. (2003). Examining language in context: The need for new research and practice paradigms in the testing of English language learners. *Educational Researcher, 32*(2), 3–13.

Southworth, G., & DuQuesnay, H. (2005). School leadership and system leadership. *Education Forum, 69*(2), 212–220.

Sperber, D., & Wilson, D. (1995). *Relevance: Communication and cognition* (2nd ed.). Oxford, UK: Blackwell Publishing.

Stecher, B., & Kirby, S. N. (2004). *Organizational improvement and accountability: Lesson for education from other sectors.* Santa Monica, CA: RAND Corporation.

Stiggins, R. J. (2002). Assessment crisis: The absence of assessment for learning. *Kappan Professional Journal.* Retrieved from http://www.pdkintl.org/kappan/k0206sti.htm

Stricherz, M. (2001). School leaders feel overworked, survey finds. *Education Week, 21*(12), 5.

Supovitz, J. A., & Poglinco, S. M. (2001). *Instructional leadership in a standards-based reform.* Madison, WI: Consortium for Policy Research in Education.

Swanson, H. L., Saez, L., & Gerber, M. (2006). Growth in literacy and cognition in bilingual children at risk for reading disabilities. *Journal of Educational Psychology, 98*(2), 247–264.

Sweeney, J. (1982). Teacher dissatisfaction on the rise: Higher level needs unfulfilled. *Education, 102,* 203–208.

Talley, W. K., & Keedy, J. L. (2006). Assessing school council contribution to the enabling conditions for instructional capacity building: An urban district in Kentucky. *Education and Urban Society, 38*(4), 419–454.

Taylor, J. (2006). The struggle to survive: Examining the sustainability of schools' comprehensive reform efforts. *Journal of Education for Students Placed At Risk, 11*(3–4), 331–352.

Thomas, W. P., & Collier, V. P. (1997). *School effectiveness for language minority students*. Washington, DC: National Clearinghouse for Bilingual Education.

Thomas, W.P., & Collier, V.P. (2002). *A national study of school effectiveness for language minority students' long-term academic achievement*. Santa Cruz, CA: Center for Research on Education, Diversity and Excellence.

Thurlow, R., & van den Broek, P. (1997). Automaticity and inference generation. Reading and *Writing Quarterly, 13*, 165–184.

Togneri, W., & Anderson, S. E. (2003). *Beyond islands of excellence: What districts can do to improve instruction and achievement in all schools*. Washington, DC: Learning First Alliance. Retrieved from http://www.learningfirst.org/publications/districts/

Tomlinson, C. A. (2001). *How to differentiate instruction in mixed-ability classrooms* (2nd ed.). Alexandria, VA: Association for Supervision and Curriculum Development.

Torgesen, J. K., Houston, D. D., Rissman, L. M., Decker, S. M., Roberts, G., Vaughn, S., Wexler, J., Francis, D. J., Rivera, M. O., & Lesaux, N. (2007). *Academic literacy instruction for adolescents: A guidance document from the Center on Instruction*. Portsmouth, NH: RMC Research Corporation, Center on Instruction. Retrieved from http://www.centeroninstruction.org/files/Academic%20 Literacy.pdf

Tyack, D. B. (1974). *The one best system: A history of American urban education*. Cambridge, MA: Harvard University Press.

Tyack, D. B., & Cuban, L. (1995). *Tinkering toward utopia: Reflections on a century of public school reform*. Cambridge, MA: Harvard University Press.

Umbel, V. M., Pearson, B. Z., Fernandez, M. C., & Oller, D. K. (1992). Measuring bilingual children's receptive vocabularies. *Child Development, 63*(4), 1012–1020.

U.S. Department of Education. (2005). *The nation's report card: An introduction to the National Assessment of Educational Progress (NAEP)*. Washington, DC: U.S. Department of Education, Institute of Education Sciences, National Center for Education Statistics.

Valdés, G. (2001) *Learning and not learning English: Latino students in American schools*. New York: Teachers College Press.

Valenzuela, A. (1999). *Subtractive schooling: U.S.-Mexican youth and the politics of caring*. New York: State University of New York Press.

Van Houtte, M. (2006). Tracking and teacher satisfaction: Role of study culture and trust. *The Journal of Educational Research, 99*(4), 247–256.

Vigil, D. (1997). *Personas Mexicanas: Chicano high schoolers in a changing Los Angeles*. Fort Worth, TX: Harcourt Brace.

Walker, E. M., & Gutmore, D. (2001). The issue of civic capacity in urban educational reform: The case of New Jersey's thirty poorest districts. *Journal of Negro Education, (71)*1/2, 60–76.

Wang, J., & Goldschmidt, P. (1999). Opportunity to learn, language proficiency, and immigrant status effects on mathematics achievement. *Journal of Educational Research, 93*, 101–111.

Ware, H., & Kitsantas, A. (2007). Teacher and collective efficacy beliefs as predictors of professional commitment. *The Journal of Educational Research, 100*(5), 303–310.

Weinstein, C. S., Tomlinson-Clarke, S., & Curran, M. (2004). Toward a conception of culturally responsive classroom management. *Journal of Teacher Education, 55*, 25–38.

Wiley, T. G. (1994). *Estimating literacy in the multilingual United States: Issues and concerns*. Washington, DC: Adjunct ERIC Clearinghouse for ESL Literacy Education.

Wolf, M. K., Kao, J., Herman, J. L., Bachman, L. F., Bailey, A. L., Bachman, P. L., et al. (2008). *Issues in assessing English language learners: English language proficiency measures and accommodation uses—Literature review* (CRESST Tech. Rep. No. 731). Los Angeles: University of California, National Center for Research on Evaluation, Standards, and Student Testing (CRESST).

Youngs, P., & King, M. B. (2002). Principal leadership for professional development to build school capacity. *Educational Administration Quarterly, 38*, 643–670.

Index

Note: An "f" or "t" following a page number refers to a figure or table, respectively

About the Author

Dr. Ray Garcia is presently professor and chair of the Department of Educational Leadership at California State University, East Bay. Before joining CSU, he served as dean of a corporate university and chief academic officer in an urban school district. He received his doctorate from the University of Houston. He has published extensively in the area of educational reform sustainability and is a noted speaker and trainer at state and national forums. Dr. Garcia is managing the Center for Research, Equity and Community Engagement, charged with disseminating research addressing root-level factors of the achievement gap in school systems. His work with school leaders focuses on approaches to sustaining school improvement efforts through the optimization of staff commitment. He has been the recipient of the University Council of Educational Administration Excellence Award and has received numerous academic and public honors. Dr. Garcia is involved in various community activities and has served on several boards.